AF560398

You Can Get It Done

Books by Liisa Kyle

You Can Change Your Life: A Workbook to Become the Person You Want to Be

Self-Worth Essentials: A Workbook to Understand Yourself, Accept Yourself, Like Yourself, Respect Yourself, Be Confident, Enjoy Yourself, and Love Yourself

Life Levers: Make Small Changes to Create Big Improvements in Your Life

Coping in Times of Crisis: Ways to Handle Uncertainty and Navigate the Unknown Future

Overcoming Perfectionism: Solutions for Perfectionists

Get Over It: Overcome Regret, Disappointments, and Past Mistakes

Overcoming Emotional Eating: Coach Yourself to Manage Cravings, Eat Mindfully, and Foster a Healthy Relationship with Food

Making the Most of 2025: A Workbook

Be More Creative: 101 Activities to Unleash and Grow Your Creativity

Making the Most of Your Retirement: Ways to Foster Health, Happiness & Fulfillment at Any Age

Know Yourself Better: Self-Discovery Questions and Activities

Coach Yourself: Self-Coaching Questions and Activities for Self-Discovery and Personal Growth

40 Ways to Enjoy Turning Forty: Make the Most of Your Milestone Birthday to Have the Best Year Ever

50 Ways to Enjoy Turning Fifty: Make the Most of Your Milestone Birthday to Have the Best Year Ever

Making the Most of Your Milestone Birthday: 52 Ways to Have the Best Year Ever

Coping with the Virus Crisis: Ways to Handle Uncertainty and Navigate the New Normal

You Can Get It Done

CHOOSE WHAT TO DO, PLAN, START, STAY ON TRACK, OVERCOME OBSTACLES, AND FINISH

Liisa Kyle, PhD

ALEPH BOOK COMPANY
An independent publishing firm
promoted by *Rupa Publications India*

Published in 2014 by Shimmer Press

Published in India in 2024
by Aleph Book Company
7/16 Ansari Road, Daryaganj
New Delhi 110 002

Cover Illustration: Shutterstock/Asiya Hotaman

ISBN: 978-81-970811-8-7

1 3 5 7 9 10 8 6 4 2

Printed in India

Contents

Contents

CHAPTER 1

How This Book Can Help You

Would you like to be more productive? What seems to be the problem?

Perhaps you are very busy—multitasking like crazy—but find you're not making enough progress on anything. Your actions seem more scattered and less effective than you would like.

Maybe you are troubled by what *isn't* getting done. Are your half-done projects causing you guilt, disappointment, or stress?

Is there something specific you want to accomplish...but you can't seem to be able to make yourself do much about it?

Maybe you have a vague sense that you should be doing *something* but you can't quite put your finger on what that is.

Perhaps you have trouble deciding what to do at a given moment. There's so much to do that you don't know where to begin or where to put your efforts. Possibly you're concerned about making the wrong choice—so you end up stuck.

Maybe you know *what* you want to do...but you can't figure out *how* to make it happen.

Is procrastination a problem for you?

When you do get going on a project, is it tough to hang in there and keep working on it? Or to keep the deadlines you set for yourself?

Do you get distracted or overwhelmed in the thick of it? Perhaps you find it difficult to manage whatever obstacles or challenges arise. Is it hard for you to get back on track when you encounter a setback?

Do you find it tough to finish that last five or ten percent of whatever you're doing?

If any of these challenges sound familiar, know that by choosing this book, you've taken a key step to finding solutions that will work for you.

I learned how to get a lot done early in life. Before I turned thirty, I had earned my Master's and PhD in Psychology from the University of Michigan. I've spent the two decades since helping people get things done, be more productive, and make better use of their time.

I've written this book so you can too. It doesn't matter what you've got going on or what you're trying to do, this book is designed to help you *get it done.*

We'll begin by taking stock of what works well for you and what does not. You can become wildly more productive and effective when you take into consideration your unique experiences, preferences, and circumstances. That will be the focus of Chapter 2.

Next, consider this basic question: are you having problems doing things in general...or are you having trouble doing something in particular?

If you have **difficulty doing things in general**, turn to Chapter 3 for 'Three Keys to Getting Things Done'. These are the essential tools to be more productive, more focused, and more efficient.

If, instead, you are **having trouble doing something specific**, what seems to be the problem?

If you can't seem to **Choose What to Do**, turn to Chapter 4 for a five-part process to figure out What You Really Want as well as proven techniques to prioritize your options.

If you're having problems formulating a plan, turn to Chapter 5 for a step-by-step guide to devise and implement a **Plan**.

If you know what you want to do but can't seem to begin, turn to Chapter 6 for Eight Ways to **Get Started**.

If you've started but are having trouble maintaining momentum, turn to Chapter 7 for Six Essential Tools to **Stay On Track**.

If you have difficulty **Overcoming Obstacles**, turn to Chapter 8.

Chapter 9 is about **Finishing**. This is where to turn if:

- You're grappling with whether or not to quit a project
- Your project ends prematurely for reasons out of your control, or
- You are having difficulty actually finishing something you'd like to complete.

◆

HOW TO MAKE THIS BOOK MOST EFFECTIVE FOR YOU

This book is designed so that you can work through the material sequentially—or, if you prefer you can hop around to whichever sections you need, when you need them.

Work through the contents at a pace that is comfortable and engaging for you, in whatever order makes sense for you. (Note that there is some repetition woven across the chapters to accommodate this flexibility. It also gives you the opportunity to apply certain techniques in a variety of circumstances.)

Each section in this book is packed with proven tools, techniques, and practical activities. You will get far more out of this book if you participate. If the activity involves answering questions, it's more powerful if you actually write (or type) them out. Once you begin jotting down responses, you will find many new insights will emerge faster and more clearly than if you simply scan the questions and assume you know how you'll respond.

If you really want to *get it done,* write out your responses.

Ready to *get it done*? Turn to the next chapter to begin.

CHAPTER 2

What Do You Know About Yourself?

Whatever it is you want to do, *you can get it done.*

Whoever you are, you have gotten things done in the past. You have gotten yourself to this point in time and accomplished many things along the way—in school, at work, at home, in your leisure time, and more. Please take a moment to do the following activity.

> ACTIVITY
>
> List at least ten things you've accomplished in your life. (For best results, actually write down your list.) Consider the following:
>
> - Things you've done of which you are proud
> - Goals you've reached
> - Challenges you've overcome
> - Problems you've solved
> - Things you've created
> - Successful relationships (personal and professional)
> - Prizes, awards, badges, certificates, diplomas, degrees, credentials, etc.
> - Key life milestones (e.g., acquiring jobs, homes)

WHAT WORKS WELL FOR YOU?

As you think about your answers to the preceding activity, consider what has worked well for you in getting these things done. Over the years, what practices, habits, or activities have you found that enhance your productivity or effectiveness?

Perhaps you've found that you need to give attention to your top priority first thing in the morning to make real progress on it. Maybe you've found a way to motivate yourself using a particular app. Perhaps you've found that taking short breaks throughout the day improves your focus.

One important clarification: The key here is to make note of **healthy** things that have worked for you. Avoid anything crazy-making or stress-inducing. Many of my clients are high achievers who can grit their teeth and power through almost anything if pressed...but they come to me because they are miserable operating that way.

Or they find that pushing themselves isn't actually effective. They might be getting things done but at an exorbitant cost to their well-being or their relationships.

Your mission is to identify ways to be productive yet healthy and happy.

ACTIVITY

MAKE A 'WHAT WORKS FOR ME' LIST

1. Read each item on your list of accomplishments. As you do, make a new list of things that helped each achievement. What has worked well for you in the past?
2. Review your answers. Cross off anything that was unpleasant or stress-inducing.
3. Now, think about your life more generally. Over the years, what practices, habits, or activities have you found that have enhanced:
    - Your happiness?
    - Your well-being?
    - Your productivity?

The point of these activities is to demonstrate that you already have some tools to get things done. You are not starting from scratch. You already know some things that work for you. Throughout this book, you'll have the opportunity to explore and test many other tools and techniques. It's up to you to discover what will work for you, given your unique preferences and circumstances.

But first a pop quiz: How many of the things on your 'Works Well for Me' lists have you done today? This week? This month?

ACTIVITY

Go through your 'What Works for Me' list. Beside each, write the approximate date when you last did it.

If it's been a while since you've done the things on your list, know that you are not alone. It seems to be a quirk of human nature. We find things that work for us—practices or habits that make us happy or healthy or productive—and then we don't do them.

We start off great guns, say, drinking an extra glass of water before each meal. We find that we feel better. We snack less. Our skin looks better. We commit to making this a regular daily practice. And for a time, we do. Then, a couple of months later, we feel parched and cranky and we realize it's been weeks since we've done this very simple thing that we know works for us.

It doesn't really matter *why* we do this to ourselves, so long as we implement some tools to short-circuit this tendency. It can be as quick and easy as reviewing your 'What Works for Me' list on a regular basis—say daily, weekly, or monthly.

Bonus points if you reward yourself for doing the things on your 'Works Well For Me' list. Why not? You're doing what you set out to do. You've earned a treat. Plus, it'll reinforce the likelihood you'll keep doing what works well for you, going forward.

ACTIVITY

1. Going forward, keep your 'What Works for Me' list handy.
2. As you find new things that work well for you (such as particular tools and techniques in this book), add them to your list.
3. How can you reward yourself for doing what you intend? Make a list of simple, easy, fitting treats you can give yourself.
4. Review your 'What Works for Me' list from time to time. Are you doing what you know works well for you?
   - If so, reward yourself.
   - If not, make whatever adjustments are needed.
5. If you ever get stuck or stalled, review your list. Remind yourself of what you'd already accomplished and what works well for you.

◆

ARE YOU A PLODDER OR A BURSTER?

Another component of understanding what will work for you is considering your own personal quirks and patterns in getting things done. For example, are you a Plodder or a Burster?

Plodders chip away at projects methodically, at a reasonable pace, generating regular, continuous output. They like chipping away at things steadily and calmly.

Bursters, on the other hand, tend to need a dormant 'percolation period' (which is really more of a teeth-gnashing, popcorn-munching, garment-rending frenzy of seemingly non-relevant activities) before finally (usually at the last moment) they generate an extraordinary amount of work—boom boom boom—in short order. Bursters thrive on adrenaline, drama, and riding emotional roller coasters.

Consider how each would approach the task of, say, writing five blog posts in a particular week. A Plodder would craft, edit, and publish one blog post every day for five days. In contrast, a

Burster will spend four days doing God knows what and then—boom!—compose and publish all five blog posts in a flurry on Friday.

(Note that you are not wed to either category exclusively. You may be a Plodder in some activities and a Burster in others.)

The point of this is that once you are aware of how you tend to operate, you can schedule things accordingly. You can do what works well for you without stress or guilt or shame. *'Yes, I'm a Burster and that's okay. It's fine if 'my process' means I need to do random activities for a bit. There's no need to freak out about that. I know whatever needs to get done will get done by deadline.'*

Here's an opportunity to play anthropologist with yourself as a subject. Observe yourself over the next few weeks and take notes on what you notice. What are your unique behavioural patterns as you go through different activities in your life?

When do you have the most energy? Under what circumstances are you happiest and most productive? What makes things easier for you?

ACTIVITY

1. Consider different projects or activities. What is your typical approach to each? Add your answers to your 'What Works for Me' list.
   - Are you a Plodder or a Burster?
   - When during the day or week do you have the most energy?
   - Under what circumstances are you happiest?
   - Under what circumstances are you most productive?
   - What makes things easier for you?
2. Keep your list handy for the next few weeks. Jot down other things you notice about how you operate.

The better you know yourself, the easier it is to be happy, healthy and productive. When you know what works well for you, it becomes much, much easier to get things done.

◆

WHAT DOES NOT WORK WELL FOR YOU?

It's equally helpful to recognize what does *not* work well for you. By becoming aware of whatever tends to interfere with your productivity, you can avoid it, going forward.

Perhaps you've noticed that whenever you succumb to the siren calls of social media first thing in the morning, you tend to get hijacked by distractions...whereas if you defer Facebook until later in the day, you get a solid block of productive work done. Maybe you know that you're apt to snack excessively when under stress...which doesn't do anything other than make you puffy and cross with yourself.

If you make note of those things you want to avoid doing and hold yourself accountable, you'll be more effective, more productive, and more content.

ACTIVITY

1. Make a list of what you know does NOT work well for you.
   - What's unhealthy or unhelpful?
   - What causes undue stress or distractions?
   - What causes you to squander energy or opportunities?
   - What challenges do you have to overcome repeatedly?
2. How can you help yourself avoid these unhelpful or unhealthy things?
   - What's worked in the past?
   - What else might you try?
   - How can you hold yourself accountable?
3. Use this information to refine your 'What Works Well for Me' list. What do you need to avoid or curtail to be pleasantly productive?

Once you have a better sense of what works well for you and what doesn't, you can apply these insights to the tools and techniques in this book.

Next, answer the question first posed in Chapter 1. You are reading this book because you are having difficulty getting things done. **Are you having problems doing things in general...or are you having trouble doing something in particular?**

If you have **difficulty doing things in general**, turn to the next chapter.

If, instead, you are **having trouble doing something specific**, what seems to be the problem?

If you can't seem to **Choose What to Do**, turn to Chapter 4.

If you're having problems formulating or implementing a **Plan**, turn to Chapter 5.

If you know what you want to do but can't seem to **Start**, turn to Chapter 6.

If you've started but are having trouble **Staying on Track**, turn to Chapter 7.

If you are having difficulty **Overcoming Obstacles**, turn to Chapter 8.

Turn to Chapter 9 if your challenge is with **Finishing**, for example:

- If you're grappling with whether or not to quit a project
- If your project ends prematurely for reasons out of your control, or
- If you are having difficulty actually finishing something you'd like to complete.

CHAPTER 3

Three Keys to Get Things Done

Sometimes people come to me for coaching because they are having trouble with a specific goal or project. More often, my clients seek me out for vaguer complaints, such as:

- *I seem to be so busy but I'm getting nothing done.*
- *I hate that I waste so much time; I'm afraid I'm squandering my life.*
- *I've got so many projects and ideas and I can't seem to make progress on any of them.*
- *I'm not making good use of my time.*
- *There's so much I want to do but I don't know how to get it all done.*

If any of that is true for you, please read on.

THE COSTS OF HAVING TOO MUCH TO DO

Do you set unrealistic expectations for what you can get done? Is your calendar/planner crammed full? Do you write such long To-do lists that whatever you do get done seems minimal compared to all there is left to do?

The tendency to over-commit yourself is understandable—you have an awful lot to do. However, it's also not particularly helpful.

There are considerable costs to this approach:

1. To-do lists foster a chronic state of dissatisfaction.
It feels awful to fall short of your ambitious plans, day after day. This can be frustrating, and stressful. You can feel hopelessness and despair, as if you are bailing out a sinking boat with a teaspoon. You can feel like a loser.

2. To-do lists make it harder to keep going.
Whenever you're feeling unproductive in the grand scheme of things, it's de-motivating. It requires more energy to start, to keep going, and to get things done. When your motivation flags you may become anxious or fearful. You might feel overwhelmed or stuck. You are likely to procrastinate and to end up wasting time.

3. To-do lists devalue whatever does get done.
No matter what you accomplish, it is dwarfed by all that remains to be done. Even a major triumph can pale next to the mountain of things left to do. There's a tendency to rush off to the next thing without adequately acknowledging your accomplishments.

4. To-do lists can throw life out of balance.
Whenever you're scrambling around, wrangling overly long To-do lists, something gets short shrift. It might be your health or your relationships. It might be your domestic responsibilities or your long-term dreams.

◆

If any of this sounds familiar, consider an alternative to lengthy To-do lists. **Often, by aiming to do less, we can get more done.**

Think about it: If you have less on your plate, you can give more and better) attention to each thing. Consider a plate filled high from an all-you-can-eat buffet—a mishmash of random items such that you end up scarfing down without tasting much of anything. There might be some delicious bits in there but they are lost in the heap. Compare this with a fancy haute cuisine dish—a few beautiful elements artfully arranged so each morsel is exquisitely prepared to delight your palate.

If you are having difficulty getting things done, it may be that your to-do list is like the all-you-can-eat buffet plate. To the extent you can edit it—delete the filler and less appetizing components—you can concentrate on the tastiest elements.

When you have less on your plate, you can give each element your full attention. You can savour it and make the most of it. Then it's a matter of figuring out how to manage your efforts in a way that you enjoy. Would you like to work your way around the plate in a systematic, clockwise fashion? Would you prefer to toggle between different elements—to focus on the meat, then savour the potatoes, then go back to the meat, for example? There are countless ways to empty your plate. It's up to you to choose.

Let me share with you what I've learned from the past two decades of coaching people to be more productive. There are three keys to getting things done:

THREE KEYS TO GET IT DONE

Key #1: Do less to get more done.
Edit what's on your plate.

Key #2: Focus on only one thing at a time.
Give your full attention to a single task at any given moment.

Key #3: Find time management strategies that work for you.

Figure out how to manage your time and efforts effectively, given your unique preferences and circumstances.

We'll devote the rest of this chapter to examining each of these in turn.

Key #1: Do Less to Get More Done

With fewer things on your plate, you can give more and better attention to each item. Here's how:

1. Prune your To-Do list.

You are a busy person. It's helpful to take stock and trim away unnecessary activities. What can you eliminate?

What are you doing that you *really* don't need to be doing at all? What needs to be done that could be done by someone else? What can you delegate? What can you hire someone else to do?

If money is an issue for you, what goods or services could you barter or trade to get things done? For example, if you love cooking but hate cleaning and a friend loves cleaning but hates cooking, could you swap chores?

Also consider what your time is worth. For example, if you can make $60/hour in your home business, does it make sense for you to cut the grass yourself if you can pay someone to do your lawn care for half that amount? Why not hire someone and spend that time generating income?

As well, consider any activities in which you may be applying excessive effort. Are there things you are aiming to do 'perfectly' that really don't have to be? Where could you aim for 'good enough' instead of 'perfect'? Could you aim for '95%' instead of '100%' to save the time and toil that last 5% is costing you?

ACTIVITY

PRUNE YOUR TO-DO LIST

Consider what's on your current to-do list:

- What doesn't need to be done at all? What can you eliminate?
- What can you do less of?
- What needs to be done but could be done by someone else?
  - What can you delegate?
  - What can you hire someone to do?
  - What goods or services could you barter to get things done for you by someone else?
- Where are you applying excessive effort? Where could you aim for 'good enough' instead of perfection?

2. Evaluate what's left on your list.

Review your To-do list with a critical eye. What is important, fulfilling, and/or enjoyable? What isn't? What's urgent and what isn't?

If you haven't already, delete or reduce all unimportant, unfulfilling, and unpleasant items on your list. If something falls in these categories but it is necessary, how can you minimize it?

Now look at what's **important, fulfilling, or enjoyable**. Urgent, important items pretty much take care of themselves…but what often gets lost are items that are important but not urgent. These are the things most influencing your productivity. This is where you will benefit from focusing your attention and time.

First things first. It's like that old story about how much you can fit in a jar. First put in the big rocks (most important, most fulfilling, most meaningful, most enjoyable items). If you want to add more, next add smaller rocks. More? Then add sand. More? Then add water. To enhance your productivity, ensure that you're attending to what's really important *first*.

Also consider the **80:20 Rule**. It's a well-established phenomenon that 'for many events, roughly 80% of the effects come from 20% of the causes.' Here's an approach by Tim Ferriss, who applies the 80:20 rule to maximizing the impact of one's efforts. For example, 'What are the 20% of customers/products/distributors that are producing 80% of the profit? Then we do the less common; we apply 80:20 to the negative: What are the 20% of activities and people that consume 80% of your time?'

Just as Ferriss focuses on the 20% of his customers that give him 80% of his sales—and 'fires' the 20% of his customers who give him 80% of his grief—you can follow suit. Rather than trying to do everything on your list, focus on the 20% projects/activities/opportunities/people that give you the most joy/success/recognition—and let go of the 20% of projects/activities/opportunities/people that are sapping 80% of your time/energy/happiness/creativity.

ACTIVITY

Consider each item on your To-do list:

- Put an 'I' beside anything important, fulfilling, or enjoyable.
- Put a 'U' beside anything urgent.
- Evaluate what's left. Can this be eliminated or reduced?
- Where can you apply the 80:20 rule?
    - What 20% projects/activities/opportunities/people give you the most joy/success/recognition?
    - What 20% of projects/activities/opportunities/people are draining 80% of your time/energy/happiness?

3. Prioritize with purpose.

Next, focus on whatever you've identified as urgent, important, fulfilling, or enjoyable. What means the most to you? Growing your business? Improving your health? Deepening your relationships? Making money? Establishing yourself? Expressing yourself? Building your legacy?

When you have a clear understanding of what means the most to you, you can better direct your talents, time, and energy.

Otherwise, it's very easy to get caught up in what's urgent. Or to choose less important tasks because they are less intimidating or because they'll fit into shorter time periods. It's much easier to reply to an email than to sit down and actually flesh out ideas for a new product...but to the extent you can remind yourself of your true priorities, you can make better use of your time and efforts.

Now, of your true priorities, which makes sense to do at this point in time? Among the available options, what would have the biggest impact, were you to do it next? Right now, is it more important for you check Facebook for the third time today...or to use these five minutes to call that prospective client?

Be as specific as possible. Let's say you want to write a novel. It's more helpful to schedule a particular time slot to 'outline my novel' or 'develop character X' or 'begin chapter two' rather than just 'write'. By being more precise about your purpose, you are more likely to make real progress and less likely to fritter away that time period, dithering aimlessly.

You can take it one step farther by identifying the consequences of the activity you've scheduled. For example, by outlining the book, it'll be easier to write. You'll know what needs to happen in what order. You'll be free to compose any particular scene or chapter out of order because you'll have a roadmap of where it will go.

Whatever you are doing, ask *why*. What is the purpose of this activity? What do want to achieve by doing it?

If you can't conjure up a purpose for a meeting, for example, you don't need that meeting. If there *is* a clear rationale for proceeding, it's helpful to sketch out exactly what you want to get done—so that you are poised and prepped to make the most of the experience.

(Another word about meetings: If you have a purpose and an agenda, follow it. If people stray, nudge them back to the task at hand. If an additional item pops up, decide to deal with it or 'park' it for action or discussion later.)

ACTIVITY

ORGANIZE YOUR TO-DO LIST WITH PURPOSE

- Prioritize according to importance.
- Be as specific as possible. What, exactly, must be done?
- Identify the purpose of each item. Why do you want to do it? (If there isn't a compelling reason, delete it.)

4. Break projects and activities into baby steps.

To the extent you can split your projects and activities into smaller pieces, the more manageable—and achievable—they become.

'Buying a home' would translate into smaller tasks such as budgeting, saving the down payment, identifying priorities for your family's needs, researching options, finding a great realtor, reviewing homes for sale, making an offer, arranging financing, arranging utilities and insurance, moving, etc.

Each of these elements can be further broken down into smaller pieces. For example, 'researching options' might involve exploring different neighborhoods, researching relevant information about each (home prices, crime rates, local schools, walkability, local amenities, etc.), reviewing online listings, and going to some open houses to learn about the local real estate market.

By slicing each of these tasks into even smaller pieces, you will get things done. 'Reviewing listings online' might translate into 'spending at least fifteen minutes a day reading online real estate listings at least four days a week.' With this formula, you are guaranteed to spend at least an hour on something that is important to your family and your goal of owning a new home. (And frankly, if you are consistently reviewing real estate listings at least fifteen minutes a day, you'll probably be compelled to spend more time than that, more often.)

Ideally, baby steps should be laughably small—so small you don't think twice about doing them. That's the whole point. When what's on your To-do lists is really, truly easy, you'll do it.

Breaking dreams or big projects into baby steps means that:

- You'll sidestep procrastination—and the guilt and stress associated with not doing what you 'should' be doing.
- You'll avoid stress and being overwhelmed. You're just doing baby steps, right? No big thing.
- You'll enjoy steady progress—which is intrinsically very motivating. It's gratifying (and fun) to get things done. It fuels your enthusiasm.
- You'll be happier. It just feels darned good to make discernible progress.
- You will be focused on the present moment—what you can do right now. This helps you avoid fretting about the future—or dwelling in the past (on regrets and disappointments).
- You'll maintain momentum over time, more easily.
- You'll be more creative. If you're chipping away on your project on a regular basis, your mind is focused on it and can play with it more. Everything you encounter can enrich your project if you are dabbling in it consistently over time.

ACTIVITY

Consider each item on your To-do list. See which items you can break down into baby steps.

The baby steps technique is a wonderful way to establish helpful or healthy habits.

If your goal is to establish a habit of walking at least an hour a day, for example, then you might begin the process by committing to walk at least ten minutes a day (assuming that sounds realistic for you).

After that becomes second nature, aim for fifteen. When that seems like old hat, go for twenty...until eventually you increase your total daily walking time to an hour.

Again, the key here is that your beginning goal should be so easy it's laughable. Going back to the last example, if walking ten minutes a day is easy as pie, that's a great place to start. If, however, it proves to be too challenging, then start with five minutes. Still too much? Begin with one or two.

It *really* doesn't matter where you start, so long as it is a baby step towards your goal. Baby steps, baby—the smaller the better.

ACTIVITY

What healthy habits would you like to start? (Make a list.)

Pick whichever of these is most important or most interesting for you right now.

What would be a laughably easy way to begin?

Baby steps work in reverse, too. Let's say you want to reduce or eliminate an unhelpful or unhealthy habit. Small changes can have big impact.

You can find a way of reducing your bad habit incrementally.

For example, if you're a pack a day smoker—that's twenty cigarettes a day.

It probably wouldn't be difficult to cut your consumption down to nineteen cigarettes a day this week, right? If that's easy, then next week, you could reduce your daily habit to eighteen... and so on.

ACTIVITY

What unhealthy or unhelpful habits would you like to curtail, reduce, or eliminate? (Make a list.)

Pick whichever of these is most important or most interesting for you to reduce or eliminate right now.

What would be a baby step in the direction you desire?

5. Identify any strategic levers that will help.

Next, take a step back and be strategic. Are there any small strategic changes you could make that would achieve what you want? This might be a small shift in thought or behaviour. It might involve a new rule or boundary.

I call these changes 'strategic levers' because they are tiny shifts in thought, word, or deed that can be leveraged into enormous changes.

Let's say you're an over-eater who snacks all day, like me. (In my case, I can actually measure how difficult an article is by how many bowls of popcorn I've consumed while drafting it.) It doesn't work to say, "Okay, from now on, I'll snack less." It doesn't work to say "I'll consume one less bowl of popcorn on each article I write."

Instead, I needed to implement a simple, small change—a strategic lever—to trick myself into snacking less. Specifically, I made a simple new rule: no more eating at my computer. If I want to snack, I have to stop work and go sit in the dining room while I chow down.

ACTIVITY

Consider each item on your To-do list. Are there any small, strategic changes you could make that will help you accomplish what you want to do?

6. Set reasonable, achievable expectations.

Rather than chronicling every single thing you could conceivably do and every item you 'should' do in a twenty-four-hour period, **focus on only two or three things per day.**

Ideally, commence each day by selecting one key task in each of two or three areas of life. Let's say, you pick whatever would be most important in your work life, in your domestic life, and for your health. For example, the most important things I could do today would be to spend at least an hour writing this chapter, to trim my dogs' nails, and to go to Zumba class.

I can sense you balking already—I can sense you judging my choices as lame and wailing, 'Maybe you can operate this way, but I have *way* too much to do!' Let me explain. Of course, I have dozens of things to do today. That's not the point.

The point is that **by setting the intention to accomplish my top priorities, they will get done.** Moreover, since they are simple, easy, concrete tasks, they will be completed without stress, muss, guilt, procrastination, gnashing of teeth, or consumption of popcorn.

Note that my priorities are simple, specific, and I know why I want to do each of them. *(Working on this chapter is my next step in completing this book; trimming my dogs' nails means they walk comfortably; Zumba class is a source of joy and fun and socializing plus it keeps me healthy.)*

Because I've selected three clear tasks that are important to me, they are likely to get done.

Further, as each of the three tasks gets done, I will earn a sense of accomplishment and gain a boost in energy. Because my choices span three different areas of life, my actions are fostering life balance.

Sound good? Here's the best part: Once these items are completed, I'm free to do more. Whatever else I do is icing on the proverbial cake. This means that whatever else I get done today, I'll feel that much better, that much more productive, that much more competent, and that much more fulfilled and satisfied.

However, if something should prevent me from doing more than these priorities today, it's okay. I won't despair or feel anxious or guilty or lazy or stressed. I've already set out what I intended for the day.

If I'm consistent over time—if I use this technique every day—I am setting myself up for **chronic success and satisfaction over time**. By definition, I'll be getting done whatever is most important in different areas of life. That's all any of us can reasonably expect to do.

Some people reject this approach because it seems lazy or too easy. It seems like 'cheating'. If this sounds like you, you may be making things more difficult for yourself than is warranted. You may be operating out of a false belief that you must struggle and toil to earn success. The truth is this: you don't. There is no legal or cosmic requirement that you must suffer to be productive. If you try doing less, you are likely to find that you get more done, more easily.

This approach may seem counter-intuitive but it works. To the extent you can ditch the lengthy To-do list and focus on only two or three daily priorities, you will get more done, with less stress, and with more satisfaction.

Understand that you will NEVER get it *all* done. You will always be generating new projects, ideas, and opportunities. There will always be other things you could do. It is unfair, if not cruel, to expect some magical moment when your behemoth To-do list will be utterly completed. It is more reasonable—and kinder—to aim for steady progress. To find contentment in what *does* get done, whatever it is.

Do yourself a favour and try the following activity right now.

ACTIVITY

Today, what is one important thing you could do for yourself? (Write it down.)

Today, what is one important thing you could do for your business, profession, career, or vocation? (Write it down.)

What is one important thing you could do for your household today? (Write it down.)

Read your answers. Remind yourself why these three things are important to you. (If you don't know, pick something else.)

Today, focus first on your chosen three priorities. Avoid tackling other activities until these three things are completed.

Repeat this process every day this week.

7. Do what's most important first thing in the morning.

Take advantage of how your brain works. Research has shown that our brains work best right after we awaken. Our minds are refreshed, replenished, and rebooted. The assaults of the day's demands and interruptions have not yet commenced. As a special bonus, there's a carryover from our dream-state that makes us more innovative and more creative in whatever we do first thing in the morning.

To the extent you can devote your very first activity of the day to whatever is most important to you, you can make significant strides more easily. Consider your top priorities, be they spiritual practices or physical activities or professional projects or personal pursuits. Imagine giving them twenty minutes (or more) of your attention first thing. (You'll be surprised what you can get done in twenty minutes if you give yourself the opportunity consistently—ideally every day.)

Postpone checking your email, phone messages, social media, or news feeds until later in the day. Avoid those sorts of distractions until *after* you've spent time doing something important to you.

As an added bonus, whatever time you can devote to your initial activity of the day—be it twenty minutes, an hour, or more—you've already accomplished something. For example, if you, say, write five pages first thing, then no matter what happens for the rest of the day, you've written five pages! Five pages a day adds up fast. Five pages a day, five days a week means a script in a month or a novel in two.

If you 'don't have time' given the practical constraints of your living situation, ask yourself, 'What would it mean if I could make efficient, regular progress on my top priority?' Would that be worth doing some creative problem solving to figure out how to get yourself twenty minutes first thing in the morning?

Yes, you've got a household to launch every morning...but can you find twenty minutes (or more) for your top priority *before* your family awakens and domestic logistics hijack your attention?

If you believe you're not a 'morning person' so there's no point trying—consider that you may be missing out on the most productive time of your day. Your biology is such that your brain works best after it's had some rejuvenating shuteye.

Merrill Markoe is an accomplished writer of television and nine books. Recently, when she was recovering from surgery, she was pretty much forced to write first thing in the morning—a practice she'd avoided throughout her professional life. She was astonished at the difference it made. Gone was the stress, self-loathing, and angsty procrastination that had plagued her for decades. It was replaced by stress-free productivity and a joy in the writing process she hadn't experienced before.

I am also a convert. I'm a life-long night owl. Never in my wildest dreams could I have imagined myself voluntarily arising at 5 a.m. But when we moved to a new city, my husband had to get up that early because of his commute. I started setting my alarm at oh-dark-thirty partly out of love (I wanted to have a coffee with him and see him off) and partly out of guilt (it didn't feel right to sleep in when he couldn't).

Once I began getting up so early, I discovered that it supercharged my productivity. Turns out the wee hours are an excellent time to work and think without interruption. It opens up my schedule to accommodate coaching clients in far-flung time zones. By breakfast time, most days, I've already accomplished my top priorities. This is incredibly freeing because for the rest of the day I can give attention to whatever I wish. I can respond flexibly to whatever unfolds.

Honestly, I would never have tried this voluntarily, but once I did, it was eye-opening. It is unexpectedly easy to get up early. It is surprisingly effortless to make real, substantial progress in those early hours, which is highly gratifying.

Why not give it a try? See what the experience is like for you. Consider your top priorities. How could you give them your attention, first thing in the morning? Maybe you just need to rearrange your activities to do more important things first, and less important things later. Perhaps you need to set your alarm clock twenty minutes earlier so you can give some uninterrupted thought to your top priority before your household arises and domestic logistics intervene. Maybe you need to organize things before you go to bed the night before.

ACTIVITY

This week, try giving your attention to your top priorities first thing in the morning. See what the experience is like for you.

8. Focus on what is getting done, rather than what isn't.

It is highly gratifying and much more pleasant to acknowledge your accomplishments than to despair over everything you have yet to do.

Also, it keeps you on track. By monitoring your progress, you can ensure that you are doing what you intend and you can make adjustments as needed.

What will work for you? What is the simplest, easiest way you can note your progress? For example, you could keep a project journal or keep track on a whiteboard.

A colleague of mine applies colourful stickers to his wall calendar to denote how many pages he writes each day.

Creativity guru Julia Cameron advocates writing a 'Ta Dah' list every evening to chronicle your accomplishments. I love this idea because it shifts focus from your 'To Do's' to your 'Ta Dah's.'

Jerry Seinfeld has a personal goal of writing at least one new joke every day. He keeps himself on track by putting a big 'X' on his calendar for every day he does so. He is highly motivated to avoid breaking his chain of X's.

My client Susan marks different coloured stars on each week's schedule to track time she spends on each of her top priorities.

She can see, at a glance, when something's getting too little attention so she adjusts her efforts accordingly.

> ACTIVITY
>
> Look at your top priorities. For each, choose how you'd like to monitor your progress.
>
> Start doing so today. Make adjustments as needed.

9. Reward yourself for what you do.

Go farther than just making note of what you are accomplishing. Reward yourself. Give yourself treats to reinforce your successes.

The challenge with rewards, however, is that many of us have a hard time actually treating ourselves. It's up to you to identify what are fitting, pleasant, reasonable, doable rewards for meeting your target. It's up to you to actually treat yourself. It's up to you to set up your rewards so they really happen when you meet your goals. It doesn't work if you promise yourself a massage a month for exercising if you don't then actually get a massage for each month that you work out.

> ACTIVITY
>
> Going forward, make a habit of identifying pleasant, fitting rewards for meeting any goals you set. Make a practice of actually rewarding yourself for your accomplishments.

Key #2: Focus on Only One Thing at a Time

If you want to get more done, do only one thing at a time. If you want to be more effective or efficient, give your full attention to whatever you're doing.

It doesn't matter how many projects, activities, and ideas you are juggling. At a given instant, you can only do one thing.

'Oh no, not me,' you may insist. 'I'm a multi-tasker. Right now, while I'm reading this, I'm also designing a new product line, listening to the news, and texting my mom.'

You may believe you are doing several things simultaneously but studies have shown that's not possible. Really what happens is that your brain toggles among those different activities every second or so. At any given instant, you are doing only one of them. Every time you switch tasks, there is a cognitive cost as your brain switches gears. (*Now where was I again?*) By toggling so quickly among different activities, you're not doing any of them particularly well. Research has proven that multi-taskers reduce their productivity by about forty percent. Forty percent!

Frankly, you're being unnecessarily hard on yourself. It's much easier to focus on one thing at a time. And here's the good news: When you stop trying to do everything at the same instant—when you focus on just one activity at a time—you will get more done, faster, more easily, with less stress.

Let me repeat that—on the off chance you're, say, texting a friend, jotting down a grocery list, and watching a DVD while you're reading this.

Seven Benefits of Focusing on One Thing at a Time

1. It's easier.
2. You'll get more done.
3. You'll get things done faster.
4. You'll get things done more easily.
5. You'll reduce stress.
6. You'll feel better.
7. You'll be more pleasant to be around.

HOW TO FOCUS

Just do one thing at a time. Give the task your full attention. That's it. When you conclude one activity, pick the next task and do it.

The more you can limit your focus to one and only one thing at a time, the better. If, however, you find it difficult to concentrate, take a moment to identify and curtail whatever distractions are interfering with your attention.

Sarah is easily sidetracked by any notifications of new emails or new social media posts. Her work is interrupted by frequent alerts of items that *really* don't need to be viewed or addressed in the instant they arrive.

Jason is easily distracted by the need to research. Even minor decisions will set him running to Google different options, which often lead to him surfing random topics unrelated to the task at hand.

IDENTIFY AND REDUCE DISTRACTIONS

What interrupts your focus? Be candid. Is it email? The phone? Internet surfing? The stacks of half-done projects piled around you? Your 'To-Do' list(s)? Instagram? Facebook? Any of the thousand apps on your phone or tablet? Other people?

Take a moment to write down what tends to interfere with you sticking to one thing at a time. Next, brainstorm ways to remove or reduce those temptations. For example, you might schedule specific time periods to check your email or to return phone calls. You could turn off your notification alerts. You could postpone your internet surfing or Facebook time until the conclusion of your workday.

Yes, you need to be able to receive and respond to texts from family members and you can't schedule when your client will call with an urgent request. Of course, it's impossible to eliminate *all* distractions *all* the time. But to the extent you can *reduce* distractions—especially the siren calls of the internet and social media—the more you will reap the benefits of focusing on one thing at a time.

ACTIVITY

1. List your favorite distractions. What tends to interfere with your focus?
2. Brainstorm ways to reduce or remove each of these distractions, given your personal situation and preferences.
   - What's worked well for you in the past?
   - What have you noticed works well for others? (If you're not sure, ask them or research options.)
   - What else might you try?

Based on my decades of coaching people to *get it done*, it's clear that most people's biggest distraction is their own mind. You sit down to do something and—Ping! Ping! Ping!—ideas pop up to interfere.

If this is a challenge for you, the next section is for you.

CAPTURE AND MANAGE YOUR IDEAS

When Vivian is writing, her attention can be hijacked by ideas and 'To Do's'. Her brain suddenly starts churning out thoughts about other blog post topics or things she needs to add to the shopping list or phone calls she needs to make. Her solution is to have a Park-It Pad next to her when she works. When ideas pop up that are unrelated to the task at hand, she jots them down, 'parking' them to be dealt with later.

You can do the same. Whenever you are doing something, be sure to have a Park-it Pad handy to capture new ideas as they occur to you. There is no reason to drop what you're doing and race off in a random direction. Instead, just jot down the disrupting thought. It's safe and you can process it later. Now resume what you were doing.

What are simple, easy ways you can capture your ideas as you go through your day? On paper—in a small notebook, index cards, or file folder? Digitally—in your computer, tablet, organizer, or phone? Tape recorders and voice mailboxes also work great and are especially useful for musicians, singers, and composers to capture auditory ideas.

Then, whenever you are working on something and new thoughts arise, you can capture them and park them for later so you're not distracted from the task at hand.

As a huge bonus, when you get in the habit of capturing and saving your ideas in a safe and easily retrievable location, you tend to generate more and better ideas.

ACTIVITY

Are you actively and consistently capturing your ideas?

If yes, make note of what's working well for you—and keep doing it. If not, commit to creating a Park-It Pad to capture your ideas.

- How, when, and where do you tend to get ideas?
- What are the best ways for you to capture your creative thoughts?

You can get even more out of your Park-It Pad if you review your ideas from time to time. It doesn't make much sense to capture your creative thoughts and organize them if you never look at them again.

Even fantastic ideas get forgotten. After publishing a bestseller, Salman Rushdie was shocked to discover in his notes that, years before, he had conjured up the exact same concept for a novel—and had completely forgotten about it.

You owe it to yourself to review your ideas periodically—[illegible], quarterly, biannually, or annually. Any hidden gems? Anything that gets your creative juices flowing? What notions have you already developed? Sometimes we get great ideas years before we have the skills or opportunity to develop them. Is there anything in your idea folders that now seems more appealing or more possible to execute than when you first captured it?

ACTIVITY

What time frame makes sense for you to have an Idea Review (e. g., quarterly, biannually, or annually)?

Go ahead and schedule your next Idea Review right now with a note to return to this page.

On that date, review the ideas you've captured.

- Are there any hidden gems?
- Is there anything that is particularly useful or appealing?
- Is there anything you'd like to implement, going forward?

Key #3: Find Time Management Strategies That Work for You

This is the crux of the matter. Once you identify your top priorities (Key #1) and are ready to focus (Key #2), the next step is to identify how best to implement your efforts. There are myriad ways to manage your time. Your mission is to figure out what works best for you, given your unique preferences and circumstances.

What follows are some fundamental techniques. As you read, consider which of these might be appropriate for your particular priorities.

Technique #1: Batching

Anyone who writes a book entitled *The Four-Hour Work Week* knows a thing or two about working efficiently and productively. In it, Tim Ferriss makes a compelling case for 'batching' together regular activities. If you check and respond to your email ten times a day, you're still doing the same amount of work as if you checked your inbox twice—but you're taking a heckuva lot more time to do it. Every time you sign into your account excessively, you're wasting time and effort. Afraid you'll miss something important if you don't check your email every hour? You won't if you set up an automatic responder to indicate your email schedule and how people can reach you for urgent matters. Something like 'Thanks for your message. I check my email at 9 am and 4 pm PST daily. If you require assistance more urgently, please contact me @ (555) 555-5555.'

Here are examples of things you can batch: checking your email, filing, making phone calls, submissions, following up on queries, laundry, weeding, etc. What are you taking too much time to do? Where are you wasting effort by repeating actions unnecessarily?

Running errands offers another batching opportunity. Rather than making separate, random trips to take care of things, group them together into one trip and plan your route to be efficient and practical.

Technique # 2: Time-Boxing

Impose time limits on things that can expand to take whatever time is available. If you know you've got to get the memo written this morning, set a reasonable deadline and stick to it. Set a timer. Hold yourself accountable.

Time-boxing is particularly important for activities you'd like to do less of. If you're a news junkie or a social media addict, put a limit on your participation. You could limit your internet surfing to, say, thirty minutes per day. This gives you permission to indulge but prevents you from over-indulging.

ACTIVITY

What would you like to be doing less of? (Make a list.)

Pick whichever of these is most detrimental for you right now.

What would be a reasonable new limit on this activity? What time limit can you commit to?

Here's another Tim Ferriss tip: Don't allow business phone calls to be open ended. You know how it goes. You answer, there's a bit of chitchat and rambling before the purpose of the call is revealed and eventually dealt with, followed by a closing chin-wag. Instead, answer the phone by saying something like, 'Hi Fred, I've got five minutes before my next meeting. What can I do for you?' Be helpful and then, after five minutes, it's time to sign off, as you already indicated. If there's more to do to deal with the matter, you can handle it via email or schedule a meeting or do whatever else makes sense.

Technique #3: Quotas

For some activities, it's helpful to set up target goals or quotas. Typically, this involves assigning yourself a minimum number of tasks to be completed within a given amount of time.

For example, many writers commit to a daily minimum of words or pages written. Business people may aim for a certain target of sales or new clients per week or per month. Dancers, musicians, and athletes may set goals for certain amounts of specified training or practice on specified days of each week.

One reason quotas can be especially effective is that they provide a minimal structure within which to operate. It's simple guiding notion rather than a complex, oppressive, 9-to-5 prison.

Quotas can motivate you do get things done while still providing you with flexibility in how or when you do so. For example, if I commit to write (at least) four articles a week, I can do them whenever I want, fitting them in among whatever else my week holds. It doesn't matter what arises in work or any other area of life...as long as a minimum of four pieces are filed by end of day Friday. I might draft them all on Monday, edit them on Wednesday, and finalize them on Friday. Or I might write one a day and polish it when possible.

Besides flexibility, another upside is that quotas tend to specify a 'minimum'. Once you accomplish your intended goal, it's intrinsically gratifying. As a bonus, if you choose to, you can do more, which can feel even better. In fact, my coaching clients often find it more motivating to assign a conservative quota that it is relatively easy...and oh so pleasant...to achieve, in part because it often stimulates them to do more—to exceed their minimum target.

Quotas have other benefits as well.

They can ensure you are actually participating in the things you wish to do. Just as they work for professional activities, they also can work for other areas of life. If you are looking to improve your nutrition, you could make a point of eating a salad every day. If you love to read, why not aim to read a book a week or a month (or whatever rate makes sense in your life situation)? If you love being outdoors but notice it's been weeks since you did so, establishing a minimum 'time outside' target can ensure you don't let this simple pleasure get forgotten amid everything else you're doing.

It's up to you to decide what's important.

ACTIVITY

What would you like to be doing more of? (Make a list.) What are you not doing enough of? (Make a list.)

Now, for each item on your list, ask yourself, 'What would be an appropriate target quota to aim for, given my life circumstances these days?' (If in doubt, aim for smaller, fewer, or easier goals.)

Also consider that quotas can motivate you to tackle activities that are less enjoyable but necessary. For example, if you don't like housework, you could set a minimum amount of time per day or per week to your chores. It's surprising what you can get done in even fifteen minutes a day. Alternatively, you could create a realistic list of minimum to-do tasks for the week.

When tackling things you don't enjoy doing, it's particularly important to choose the smallest, easiest, most conservative quota possible. If your target is too ambitious, you won't do it and you'll feel worse about it. If in doubt, aim for less.

ACTIVITY

What necessary activities do you find it difficult to make yourself do? (Make a list.)

Now, for each item on your list, ask yourself, 'What would be the smallest, easiest, most conservative target quota I could aim for, given my life situation?'

Quotas can be reinforced and enhanced with rewards. While meeting quotas is intrinsically gratifying, you can solidify your preferred behavioural patterns by rewarding yourself with actual treats whenever you meet your quotas.

ACTIVITY

What is a quota you'd like to establish?

What would be a pleasant, fitting and doable reward you would enjoy when you meet your goals?

How can you put this in place so it actually happens? How can you hold yourself accountable for rewarding yourself?

Will quotas work for you? It depends on the nature of your activities, your personality, your situation, and your personal preference.

Reflect for a moment. Have quotas worked well for you in the past? Are you using them currently? If not, might it be an opportunity to reinstate them? Do they need any tweaking?

If quotas have not worked well for you in the past, ask yourself, why not? For example, were you overly ambitious in your targets or time frames? Were your targets too complex or numerous for your schedule? Would a more conservative approach work better for you?

If you haven't yet tried using quotas, give them a try. See to what extent they can help you get more done.

Technique #4: Take Breaks to Get More Done

It may seem counter-intuitive, but one of the best ways you can get more done is by taking breaks in whatever you're doing. Rather than tiling the floor for four hours straight, for example, insert short breaks into your activity. Take short breaks and your body and your brain will thank you.

You'll thank yourself, too. By taking short breaks:

- You'll sidestep the feeling of being overwhelmed
- You'll keep your energy higher and avoid fatigue
- You'll avoid procrastinating

- You'll maintain clearer focus and avoid distractions more easily
- You'll allow space for 'mental magic' to happen. Brief breaks can give the 'back burner' of your brain a chance to generate an innovative solution to a problem or 'aha' ideas
- You'll get more done
- You'll find yourself less stressed and healthier
- You'll find your work is more focused and of higher quality

Bonus #1: Mini-breaks are really built-in rewards for a job well done. This is highly motivating.

Bonus #2: Using this technique makes it easier to do more, more effectively. It can increase your productivity tremendously.

So, what's the catch? There must be a catch. Actually, there are two.

Catch # 1:

For these mini-breaks to have the desired effect, you need to do them every hour of focused activity and you need to restrict them to five to ten minutes maximum.

We'll address the specifics of time management shortly, but for now the point is to commit to a pattern of alternating periods of focused work with mini-breaks.

A timer is an easy way to maintain this new rhythm. For example, you could set a timer to commit fifty-five minutes of work followed by a five-minute break.

The challenge is that you really must pause your work when the timer goes off—even if things are really humming for you.

And you really must end your break when the timer goes off or else you're just defeating the purpose of the break you're taking.

Catch # 2:
There are 'good breaks' and 'not-so-good breaks'.

'Good breaks' include things like stretching, meditating, mindful eating, physical activity (yoga, jumping jacks, crunches or walking around the block), cuddling your pet, listening to a great song, or enjoying a cup of tea. Things that are pleasant, peaceful, and a change from your major activity are ideal—and this will be unique to you and the task at hand. Writers need to take a break from sitting at the keyboard whereas gardeners need to rest their bodies. Parents may need some quiet time whereas kids may need to run around and burn off some energy.

'Not-so-good breaks' include any stressful activity (like calling the cable company), any multitasking (trying to cram umpteen things into your break), or anything difficult to stop after just five minutes (e.g., computer games or chatting with a friend). Again, this is highly individualized.

KEY QUESTIONS

1. What are healthy, helpful, peaceful five-minute breaks for you? (Make a list.)
2. What would be unhealthy or unhelpful breaks for you? (Make a list.)

HELPFUL DAILY PRACTICE: FIVE-MINUTE BREAKS EVERY HOUR

When you are engaged in an intense or stressful activity, use a timer to ensure you give yourself five-minute breaks every hour.

Choose from your list of healthy, helpful, and/or peaceful activities listed above.

Avoid the unhealthy or unhelpful activities you identified above.

Technique #5: The Magic Hour Method
This technique is simple. Devote an hour a day to pursue one

particular project, goal, activity, or talent.

You'd be amazed at what you can accomplish in sixty minutes a day—and how fast sixty daily minutes can yield substantial progress. Yes, you can find that new home. Yes, you can launch a local band. Yes, you can patent that product. Yes, you can learn Italian. What's your biggest dream? You can probably accomplish it in an hour a day.

How is that possible? Well, for one thing, 'An Hour a Day' means you're actually spending time on your priority project. If you can consistently spend at least sixty daily minutes on the task, you will make steady progress towards your goal, whatever it is.

Second, it's *only* an hour a day. If the project is truly important to you, you will find an hour a day to spend on it.

An hour a day? It's doable. Speaking for myself, I can waste *much* more than an hour each day doing things that don't really matter—surfing the 'net or watching DVDs or puttering around the house. I'm happy to replace sixty of those minutes with something that's actually important to me. You can do the same. What is your own biggest time waster? Wouldn't you rather spend it on something that matters to you?

This approach is called the Magic Hour Method for several reasons:

1. You can accomplish a lot very efficiently.

The tinier steps you take, and the more often you take them, the more progress you will see.

2. It helps you focus.

'Yikes! I only have an hour to do this thing I really want to do!' Poof! Go typical distractions, excuses, and procrastination.

3. It feels magical.

It's freeing and soothing and gratifying to devote your attention to something you care about. It lifts your spirit and generates joy.

4. It enhances other aspects of your life.
When you actually give yourself time to devote to what you care about, it gives you energy. You have more oomph to tackle everything else in your life—and you do so with less resentment because you are no longer being a martyr to your responsibilities.

Hey, it's only an hour a day. Why not give it a try and see how it works for you?

THE MAGIC HOUR METHOD

1. Select a project, talent, activity, goal, task, or dream.
Pick something. Anything.

2. Begin today.
Yes, really. What's the first thing you need to do to accomplish the thing you've chosen? Just start doing it.

Work at least an hour on it. By this I mean good quality, focused work. No interruptions. No distractions. No shifting gears to other activities.

If you have difficulty focusing, try setting a timer for sixty minutes. Do as much as you can before the buzzer goes off.

3. Keep track.
When you complete today's session, pull out your favourite calendar (paper or electronic). On today's date, mark a star, a checkmark or some other sign that you put in at least one hour of quality, focused work. You can spend more time if you wish—just be sure to keep track of every day that you spend at least an hour on your chosen project.

4. Reward yourself with a 'good break'.
After each hour you spend on your priority, do something pleasant, healthy, and easy. (Here's where your list of healthy, helpful breaks can be handy.

5. Tomorrow, repeat steps 2 to 4.

6. Keep going.

Option A: Repeat each day (i.e., seven days per week), keeping an unbroken chain as long as you can. Just like Jerry Seinfeld writes a joke a day, no exceptions.

Option B: Select a day off per week so you you're spending at least an hour a day on your top project six times during the week.

Option C: Aim to do your Magic Hour at least five days a week.

Option D: Aim to do your Magic Hour at least four days a week.

Option E: Aim to do your Magic Hour at least three days a week.
Which of these options is reasonable and doable, given your unique life?

NOTE: I recommend aiming for an hour a day because it's enough time to make substantial progress. If you are consistent, your efforts will add up quickly. HOWEVER, it could be that you can't swing sixty minutes, given your life situation. **Do what makes sense for you.** Try thirty minutes a day instead. Or fifteen minutes a day. Or ten minutes. Or even five. The actual amount of time per day doesn't really matter. ***If you keep at it, you will make progress.*** If you put in five minutes a day consistently, you will get there eventually. It will take longer than if you had sixty minutes a day to devote to your chosen task but you ***will*** arrive at the same destination.

The Magic Hour Method is particularly helpful for making progress on those things you'd love to be doing, but aren't because life seems to get in the way.

It's also a way of overcoming any guilt. It's only an hour a day. Given everything you have on your plate and all the time you devote to doing things for others, you deserve to give yourself time to do what's important to you. Anyone who loves you wants you to be happy and healthy. Anyone who truly loves you would prefer that you take an hour a day to do what's important to you—instead of having you be resentful or grumpy or miserable or acting like a martyr because you have zero time for yourself.

Technique #6: Schedule

Most people are more productive when they assign particular tasks or activities to particular times. What about you? Think about times in your life when you scheduled your activities and compare them to times you didn't. Which did you find more fruitful?

Some people find scheduling doesn't work for them because they tend to overdo it. They try to cram in every conceivable thing and pre-plan every possible moment and, as a result, set themselves up for failure.

To schedule effectively, you need to apply the concepts we've explored in this chapter:

- Prioritize your activities
- Set reasonable, achievable expectations
- Do your most important tasks first thing in the morning

Ideally, sketch out the week ahead. First block out your existing commitments, including practicalities like travel time, meals, and domestic responsibilities.

Now consider your top priorities. When can you give them your attention? In particular, are there free periods of time first thing in the morning? If so, assign whatever's most important to you then.

Go ahead and make commitments to yourself. Schedule reasonable time periods that you know you can devote to the activities you've selected. If in doubt, do less.

Now review your week's plan, overall. Is it doable? Is there empty space to allow for downtime and life to intervene? If not, make adjustments. Aim for a happy balance such that your schedule is motivating but not stress-inducing. ('Yes! I can do this!' rather than 'Omigod how am I going to make it through everything?')

ACTIVITY

This week, try scheduling.

At the end of the week, assess how the experience was for you.

- To what extent were you productive?
- Were your expectations reasonable and achievable or were they overambitious?
- Going forward, what adjustments would you make to your schedule to be more effective?

If you resist scheduling yourself because you don't want to be constrained, this next technique is for you.

Technique #7: The Unschedule

In his classic book *The Now Habit*, Neil Fiore offers a nifty technique to get more done in less time. Instead of pre-scheduling what you plan to do when, start with a blank slate and fill in your calendar with what you actually do.

Create a grid with your week broken into thirty-minute periods. This is your Unschedule.

Consider your top priority. Ask, 'When can I start?'

When you start, commit to a thirty-minute block of focused, quality work. At the end of that time, record what you did on your Unschedule. Of course, you can work for more than thirty minutes, and you probably will. The point is to give yourself credit for every thirty-minute increment you do by recording it on your Unschedule.

This way, your day starts with a blank grid and fills up with evidence of your productivity, with each thirty minutes of focused, quality work.

The other key element in this approach is built-in guilt-free play. You are required to reward yourself for your productivity.

Ideally, choose (and preplan) some fun activities as treats for whatever you get done.

If scheduling doesn't work for you, try the Unschedule. Here's how:

THE UNSCHEDULE (NEIL FIORE)

1. Make your Unschedule.
Create a grid of your week with each day broken down into thirty-minute increments.

2. Schedule your Guilt-Free Play.
Select some things you really would enjoy doing this week, such as lunch with a friend, yoga class, seeing that new movie.
Block out time for these in your Unschedule.

3. Ask, 'When's the next time I can start?'

4. Start.
Aim for at least thirty minutes of focused, quality work. Avoid interruptions, distractions, or multitasking.

5. Record the work you complete on your calendar.
Document each thirty minutes of quality work you do.

6. Enjoy your guilt-free play.
Make a point of actually indulging in your free time. You've earned it.

Technique # 8: Make Better Use of Downtime

Downtime can be expected or unexpected. It can occur for brief or prolonged periods of time. It might be self-imposed or caused by things out of our control. Whatever the kind of downtime, it's helpful to give some thought to how you'd like to use it.

If you know you're going to encounter some downtime, it's easy enough to make the most of it. Let's say you have to go to the DMV or the doctor's office or somewhere else where you *know* you're going to have to wait. You have a choice about how to spend that time. You could do 'something productive'—make some phone calls or read or catch up on your email or attend to small, portable tasks on your To-do list. You could do 'something fun'—like people watching or doodling or playing games on your phone or tablet. You could do 'something relaxing'—you could sit there, doing absolutely nothing. Or daydreaming. Or meditating. Or jotting down things for which you're grateful.

How to choose what to do? Do what makes sense for you at that moment. If you're tired, relax. If you're bored or stressed, play. If you're feeling a hankering to get something done, do so. Do whatever you'd really love to do.

The trick is to be proactive about your choice. It's fine to do 'nothing'—as long as that's your intention. Otherwise, it won't feel good. Instead, it will evoke the agony of 'wasted' time.

The other trick is to make your decision as quickly as possible. It's not helpful to spend those five or ten minutes in the waiting room agonizing over your options. Pick something—anything—and do it.

If you don't already, make a new practice of preparing for possible downtime. When you think you might have a lull, give some thought to the best use of that time. *(Oh, I have to drop by the post office—I'll bring my sketch pad so I can doodle if there's a long queue.)*

Preparing for possible downtime now also prepares you for when you find yourself with time to kill when you ***don't*** expect it.

ACTIVITY

Right now, answer the following:

- If I have ten or so spare minutes, what would be productive? (List at least five things.)
- If I have ten or so spare minutes, what would be fun? (List at least five things.)
- If I have ten or so spare minutes, what would be relaxing? (List at least five things.)

Now capture your answers on an index card or in your phone so you always have it handy. The next time you find yourself with unexpected downtime, refer to your lists, take no more than five seconds to select an activity and do it.

It's up to you to manage your downtime, however it arises. If you are planning to take off a few minutes, or an evening, or a month, you can give thought to how best to use it, based on what's going on with you. It's helpful to consider not only *what* you'd like to do, but *why*.

Be strategic and purposeful about the downtime you choose to take. For example, you could reward yourself for good work with guilt-free play. You might use downtime to get more balance in your life—to take care of your health or your family.

If you're burned out, you could use downtime to refresh and recharge.

If you're stressed, you could use downtime to relax or otherwise soothe yourself.

When you think about the purpose of this particular downtime, it'll narrow down which activities are most helpful at this time.

It's just as important to consider how you *don't* want to spend this time. If you're fatigued, it's better to choose to nap for an hour than to spend the time frantically internet surfing or cleaning the kitchen or downing a pint of ice cream.

If you foresee a prolonged period of downtime, you can brainstorm your options proactively and act accordingly. Let's say you're planning a holiday. Why not embrace it as a chunk of welcome, expected downtime? Make of it whatever you wish.

Ask yourself the following: How would I like this period of time to be? What would I like to do? *(E.g., relax, east tasty treats, explore somewhere new.)* What can I learn? What new things can I try?

Equally importantly, what would I like to avoid doing? *(E.g., I choose not to fret, stress, or worry. I prefer to avoid thinking about work or situation X or person Y. I'm putting all that on pause for the duration.)*

When you are deliberately taking time off, be sure to park any guilt, misgivings, or other unhelpful thoughts that will disrupt your downtime. What good is a day off if your mind is in the office? What good is a week away when you spend it dreading whatever it is that'll be awaiting you when you return?

ACTIVITY

The next time you are planning to take some downtime, take a few minutes to answer the following:

- What do I need at this time?
- What would I like this period of time to be?
- What would I like to do? Why?
- What would I not like to do during this time?

It's a little different when you find yourself in the midst of unexpected, prolonged downtime. We'll talk about this in more detail in Chapter 8, but for now consider a situation in which you find yourself being unproductive.

The first step is to **recognize** downtime when it occurs. Maybe your computer implodes or the power goes out or you break your arm. *(Um, guess I'm done for the next while.)* Perhaps you're affected by some personal situation or professional source or stress that is hampering your productivity. *(The Jones account is in peril. I must pause progress on what I thought was my top priority.)* It might be that you find yourself in a strange new situation. It may take a while to get back up to speed. If you lose your job or a loved one, for example, you need to allow yourself time to react and recover.

Above all else, when you do recognize that you're being unproductive, avoid beating yourself up about it. Thoughts such as 'Arrgh! I've done nothing for two days! I'm a lazy good-for-nothing' are not helpful. Instead, pat yourself on the back for noticing. Better to have lost two days than three or more. Now that you recognize what's going on, you can move forward.

If there is something you can do to change the situation, do it.

If not, **accept** it. Accept the situation. Accept that this period will be less productive than you'd like. Re-adjust accordingly.

Ask '**What can I do to make the best of this situation?**' Right now, having recognized this period of downtime, what makes sense for me? What can I reasonably accomplish? What would be better to postpone? Is this an opportunity to do something else? *(Okay, I've broken my arm and I can't type. Here's a chance to try dictation software.)*

Prolonged downtime—expected or not—is a wonderful opportunity to learn something new. To try new activities without expectation—'just for fun.'

It's also a way to adjust the balance in your life. If you've been working too hard, it's a chance for R & R—and to reconnect with folks you care about. If you've been neglecting your health, you can give it some attention.

The point is, once you realize you're going to have some downtime—if you find yourself in the middle of it—it's better to make a choice about how you want to use the time at hand. Be strategic. Be kind to yourself. Use downtime as a way of giving yourself what you need at the time.

◆

FINDING WHAT WORKS FOR YOU

Reading about different time management techniques is not enough. If you want to *Get it Done*, you need to try the different options to figure out what works well for you in what circumstances.

I encourage you to spend the next month or so testing different options.

ACTIVITY

Take a few moments to examine your To-do list. Also consider the activities in your week that you know you must do (e.g., domestic chores) or that you know you will do (e.g., surfing the internet).

- Which tasks can you batch?
- Which can you time box?
- Which activities might be well managed by quotas?
- Which are prolonged activities that would benefit from regular mini-breaks?
- Which can you schedule?
- For which might you use the Magic Hour Method or the Unschedule?
- How can you make better use of your downtime?

This month, test-drive the different techniques. What works well for which activities? What doesn't? Add notes to your 'What Works for Me' list.

CHAPTER 4

Choose What to Do

This chapter is for those who haven't really figured out what they want to do, acquire, or accomplish—as well as those who have difficulty prioritizing.

What do you *really* want? If you aren't sure or can't decide, please read on. If you already know, please skip ahead to the next chapter.

CREATING YOUR VISION

Perhaps you have a vague sense of dissatisfaction and you can't quite figure out what would make you happy. Maybe you are yearning for 'more peace' or a 'better life' but you haven't yet identified the specifics.

The not-necessarily-grammatically-correct word for figuring out what you really want is 'Visioning'—and while the term may be awkward, it's also tried and true. To the extent you can create a clear picture of what you want, you can make the journey in that direction easier, faster, and more pleasant.

Beginning on the next page is a comprehensive, five-part process designed to create your own personal Vision of what it is you really want. (It's also a lot of fun.)

VISIONING ACTIVITY: PART 1

Designate a journal or digital file to capture your 'Vision Ideas'.

Clear some uninterrupted time. Pretend that it is **ten years from today** and you are pleased and proud of your life. Close your eyes, take a few deep breaths, and really feel like your life is peachy as it could be. Now, jot down as many details as you can:

- What is your life like?
- Describe what your typical day is like.
    - Where are you?
    - What are you doing?
    - Who are you with?
    - What activities are you doing?
- What have you accomplished over the past ten years? What's happened between now and then?

Keep your responses handy over the next week. As new ideas occur to you, add them.

Be sure to take a break at this point. This allows your mind to create other ideas in the background. Do something else for fifteen minutes, or an hour, or a day, or a week, or whatever time frame makes sense to you.

When you are ready to resume Visioning, return to the next activity to continue.

VISIONING ACTIVITY: PART 2

In a separate session, clear some uninterrupted time to resume your Vision Ideas. Answer each question repeatedly for as long as new responses arise. When your ideas slow down to a pause, move onto the next question.

- If a miracle occurred overnight and your life was perfect, what's the first thing you would notice? What else would you notice? *(Keep going...what else?)*
- What's on your Bucket List? What experiences would you like to

have during your lifetime?

- When you were a child, what came easily to you? What was as easy as breathing?
- When you were a kid, what was fun for you?
- What have been the most fulfilling activities and experiences in your life so far?
- What are your purposes in life? *(Yes, you have more than one.)*
- What gives you energy?
- What drains your energy?
- What makes you feel more like yourself?
- If you knew success was guaranteed, what would you do?
- If you had a billion dollars, what would you do with it?
- What legacy would you like to leave the world?

Keep your responses handy over the next week. As new ideas occur to you, add them to your lists.

Again, it's essential to take a break before proceeding with the next part of the activity. You've just done some deep thinking so give your brain something else to do for a while. When you are ready to resume Visioning, return here to continue.

VISIONING ACTIVITY: PART 3

Resuming your Vision Ideas, brainstorm at least ten things you'd really love to do. Write quickly without judging or editing your responses. It doesn't matter if they are big or small, outlandish or impractical, selfish, or silly, or anything else. Consider things such as:

- As-of-yet unfulfilled dreams
- Important goals
- Activities that would be fulfilling and gratifying
- Healthy habits you'd like to start
- New things you'd like to learn
- New skills or talents you'd like to acquire
- Activities, projects, or goals that would improve your life

- Projects already in progress
- Paused or stalled projects you would like to finish

Keep generating ideas. If you get stalled, re-read the bullet points above to see what new ideas they prompt.

Guess what? Time for another break. As covered in Chapter 3, taking breaks is a key way to get more done and to get higher quality results. When you're ready to resume, turn to the next activity.

VISIONING ACTIVITY: PART 4

In a separate session, re-read your answers to the preceding three activities. Circle the elements that are most important.
After you do, answer these questions:

- All things considered, what do you really want?
- Right now, at this point in time, what is most important?
- What would be the most gratifying?
- What would be the most pleasant? Pick a few items that jump out at you.

Designate a fresh page in your Vision Ideas journal or electronic file to capture the key elements of your Vision. Expand them. Refine them. Add more detail. If you wish, add colours, sketches, or images to embellish your ideas.

Now that you've captured the essence of your Vision, it's helpful to find ways to keep these ideas prevalent in your life. That's the purpose of the fifth and final part of the Visioning Activity. When you're ready to proceed, please turn to the next activity.

VISIONING ACTIVITY: PART 5

Create a shorthand list of the key elements of your Vision on an index card or sticky note or a memo in your phone—somewhere handy where you will see them often.

Create folders—both electronic and paper—to keep ideas pertaining to your Vision Ideas. Keep watch for relevant articles, images, and add them to your folders as you find them. As new ideas come to you, add them.

Many people enjoy creating Vision Boards as a visual representation of their Vision Ideas. If that's appealing to you, gather a posterboard, glue, scissors, and a stack of old magazines. Flip through magazines and pull out whatever images, words, and phrases represent your Vision. Affix them to the posterboard in a pleasing way. Feel free to embellish your collage with handwriting, doodles, stickers, or other art supplies. Have fun with it. Put it somewhere you will see often.

Generating Vision Ideas is fun and exciting. It's uplifting. It gives us hope for a pleasant future.

It can also be a bit scary and overwhelming. *Omigod, I've got all these ideas! What am I supposed to do now? What should I do next?*

We can make it very complicated. We can spend ridiculous amounts of time and energy researching options. Often people experience 'decision paralysis'—they've got so many options, they have difficulty choosing among them for fear of picking the wrong thing.

The solution is to prioritize.

PRIORITIZING: HOW TO CHOOSE WHAT TO DO NOW OR WHAT TO DO NEXT

1. Set a time limit on decision making.

When you are choosing among options, set a time limit, then do the best you can in the time you've allotted. A timer is a particularly effective tool to overcome unhelpful dithering. Set a timer and make a choice.

2. Identify your options.

If you've completed the Visioning Activity, examine the key

elements of your Vision. What projects or activities are possible at this point in time? Make a list.

If you haven't chosen to do the Visioning Activity, simply make a quick list. What are my options? What can I do now? What could I do next?

3. Prune your list.

Review your list. Is there anything on your list that makes you feel down or de-energized? If so, cross it off. For whatever reason, now is not the time to pursue that option. Does anything seem more like a 'should do' than a 'get to do'? Cross it off.

4. Assess what remains.

There are many ways to do this. How you evaluate your options depends on your current situation and your purpose in choosing among these options at this time.

For example, if you've been killing yourself with overwork, struggling and toiling, you might ask, 'Which of these options will be the easiest for me?'

If you're feeling down and dissatisfied with your life, you might ask, 'Which of these options would be the most fun for me?'

If you're bored, you might ask, 'Which of these options would be the most exciting for me?'

If you're feeling underutilized, you might ask, 'Which of these options will allow me to stretch and grow?'

If you're feeling unfulfilled, you might ask, 'Which of these options would be most gratifying?'

If you're not sure, ask, 'Which of these options is most important to me?'

5. Choose.

Did the preceding step pinpoint what you want to do? Excellent. Move ahead to Step 5.

If it didn't—if you have several options competing to be your top priority—here are four ways to choose among them.

- **Consider the consequences.**

Write out the potential consequences, costs, and benefits of each option, were you to pursue it.

For each option, circle the best and worst consequences and ask yourself, 'Okay, if this happens, how significant is that?'

If there is a major negative impact of a decision, then clearly you would do better to choose another option. Similarly, if there is a major benefit to Option A over other alternatives, then you'd pick Option A.

If there is little difference, then for each item ask, 'What will this mean to me in ten years?'

- **Go with your gut.**

If you're all tied up in knots and find yourself equally able to forge a rationale for—or against—every possible option, your brain is getting in the way. Forget logic. As you consider your options, what do your instincts say?

Weigh each option, one at a time. Pretend that's your choice. How do you feel? If you feel 'meh' or disappointed or dread, try the next option. If you feel happy and excited, you've found your current priority.

- **Rate your options.**

Alternatively, apply math. Assign each option a number between one and ten that represents how much you want to do it. Whichever gets the highest number is the option you choose.

If two options get the same numerical rating, here's a technique from Yvonne Oswald to break the tie. Ask, 'Which would do me the most good, this or that?' then quickly assign a number to each option.

For example, 'Between one and ten, which would do me the most good: working on my novel or designing a new website?' Then quickly—almost without thinking—give each one a grade. 'Novel, 6; Website, 8. OK, website it is.' Whichever one gets the higher number is the option you choose.

- **Let fate decide.**

If you still can't decide, write each option down on separate pieces of paper. Fold up the papers and mix them up. Pick one. That's your priority. Does your gut concur? Are you excited? Excellent! Proceed to Step 5.

If, however, you find yourself mildly disappointed, then pick a different piece of paper. Feel better? If so, proceed to Step Three. If not, try again until your gut does somersaults of joy letting you know that yes!—you got your number one choice.

(I know this paper-picking technique sounds flaky but it's the best way I know to help your intuition override your over-active brain. The goal here is to let your gut and your heart transmit information that is so easily masked by your clever brain's rationalizations.)

6. Identify first steps.

Brainstorm what you could do to initiate progress on your top priority. 'If I wanted to do [my top priority], the very first thing I could do would be...'

The smaller, the better. The easier, the better. The more doable, the better.

The idea here is to assign yourself a few simple tasks to start you on your way. That's all you have to do: start.

For example, if your top priority is to get a college degree, a first step might be to spend fifteen minutes online, researching course catalogues and admissions requirements. Note that you are not necessarily applying...you are simply looking at some options. You could stop reading and do this right now.

As soon as you select some first steps towards your top priority, you begin to make it real and you increase the probability of making real progress.

7. Test yourself.

Drop everything and spend at least fifteen minutes on your top priority. RIGHT NOW.

Why are you still reading? You chose this book to help you *get it done.* Here's your chance. Go do something to advance your top priority. Then return here.

8. Check your results.

Did you spend at least fifteen minutes on your chosen activity? Huzzah! You've found your top priority and, even better, you've begun! You're on your way. Kindly proceed to the next chapter.

Unless of course, you haven't. If you weren't able to make yourself spend fifteen minutes on what you identified as your top priority, it's time to ask, 'Is this *really* my top priority?' Be candid.

If you couldn't spend fifteen minutes on it, it is unlikely that this is your true top priority. No problem. Return to Step 4 and choose something else. And congratulations! You just saved yourself a lot of time, effort, and heartache by avoiding something that really wasn't important to you.

◆

Once you have selected your top priority, it behooves you to plan your course of action. The next chapter explains why and how.

CHAPTER 5

Planning

Once you've selected from among the many available options and decided on a particular task or project, there are many benefits to charting a specific course of action.

Why bother?

NINE SURPRISING REASONS WHY YOU SHOULD PLAN—AND TWO POTENTIAL TRAPS

1. Planning will organize you, your ideas, and your actions.
Taking time to sketch out what needs to happen, in what order, provides a framework for your future efforts.

All that's required are broad brush strokes—a skeleton around which to flesh out your game plan. For some projects, this might take ten minutes of focused thinking. Others may require days (or more) to sort out. That's okay. The moments you invest now will save you much more time later.

2. Planning reduces stress.
Planning gives you peace of mind. Once you understand what has to happen, in what order and by when, you will understand how best to direct your efforts.

Author and consultant David Allen helps his clients get organized by having them write each To-Do task, every idea, even their 'Someday/Maybe' items on separate pieces of paper. Once everything is written down, the pieces of paper are physical objects that can be prioritized and organized. His point is that when everything is written down, you know it's captured, so you can relax and simply do what's needed.

3. Planning will get you started.

Once you've thought about the overall project, there is likely to be the mental equivalent of a neon sign pointing to what needs to happen first. Having sketched out the whole process, you are likely to be raring to begin. This is far preferable to the situation in which you sit paralyzed, overwhelmed by random ideas, with no idea of what to do, let alone what to do first.

4. Planning will keep you going.

By planning, you can identify specific milestones on your way toward a specific goal. This way you can monitor your progress and reward yourself accordingly. This will help keep you on track.

5. Planning helps you handle obstacles.

As part of your planning process, you can identify possible obstacles, and brainstorm how you might deal with them should they arise. Then when your project is actually underway, you'll be more prepared for whatever unfolds.

6. Planning can give you a boost when you need it.

When your motivation flags or life intervenes, you can refer to your plan to remind yourself what you're doing, why you're doing it, and what needs to happen next. When you step back and look at your original game plan, you'll realize how much you've already accomplished, you'll remember your fundamental motivation, and you'll rekindle your initial excitement about the project.

7. Planning gives you flexibility.

If you know the overall game plan, it is easy to make the adjustments required along the way.

Say, for example, your goal is to finish that quilt by devoting at least thirty minutes a day to the project. Now let's say something happens at work so you are required to work unexpected overtime. Or you sprain your hand. Or your in-laws descend for a surprise visit. You can attend to any of these, safe in the knowledge that these few days can be easily made up on your schedule. No biggie—providing you add five extra minutes of sewing here and there so you can still reach your overall goal. It's easy enough to sew for thirty-five minutes (instead of the target thirty) for a few days to get you back on track.

8. **Planning increases the likelihood that you'll actually finish what you start.**

It's not a guarantee—but it sure can help. You've made a plan, you've monitored your progress, and you've adjusted it as needed. With each of these actions, you are increasing the probability you will accomplish what you set out to do.

9. **Planning increases your creativity.**

It is one of life's great ironies that structure begets creativity. When you create a framework within which to operate, you unleash boundless creativity within those borders. (And if you choose to colour outside the lines, that's fine too.)

Despite all these benefits, planning does carry with it a few possible problems:

Trap # 1: You spend too much time and energy planning and too little doing.

It's fine to get excited about refining your plan, but sometimes people get hijacked by the details or sucked into a vortex of never-ending research.

After you establish a broad framework, it's important to actually start the project, rather than filling in every conceivable eventuality. Set yourself a time limit beyond which you *must* move into action.

Trap #2: You become so wedded to your plan you have difficulty adjusting it as events unfold.

A good plan is flexible, not rigid. As good as your plan is, life is likely to intervene. It's better to adapt your plan as needed, rather than abandon it, or worse, cling to an inappropriate course of action simply because it was part of your original blueprint.

◆

If you avoid these traps, planning can be a godsend to getting things done.

ACTIVITY

Review the list of benefits of planning. Circle which are most important for you.

Think about projects you've planned. Also consider the planning process itself:

- What has worked well for you?
- What hasn't?
- What would you do next time to avoid the things that didn't work well?
- Have you been susceptible to either of the two potential traps? If so, what can you do to avoid them in the future?

◆

HOW TO PLAN YOUR PROJECT: A STEP-BY-STEP GUIDE

To get the most out of this chapter, I encourage you to actually work through the process using the item you selected as your top priority in Chapter 4. It might be the completion of a particular project or the learning of a new skill or starting a new healthy habit. For our purposes, let's call all of these things 'projects'.

(If you didn't go through prioritization process, no worries, just pick something—anything—you'd like to plan.)

Here's a step-by-step guide:

1. Designate a place to capture your plan and project ideas.
This might be in a project journal, in an electronic file on your computer or tablet, or in a combination of the two. Some people like using a large piece of butcher paper to make a visual version of their plan they can hang on their wall.

Record your ideas in a manner that works best for you. If a particular method worked well for you in the visioning activity in Chapter 4, use that.

Ideally, keep all your planning and project notes together in a convenient, easily retrievable location. Some people designate a computer folder containing relevant computer files (e.g., 'Project Plan,' 'Project Ideas,' 'Resources,' 'To-do,' etc.). Others prefer to work things out on paper, for example, using an accordion file to contain a project journal and folders of relevant ideas, topics, and clippings.

2. Define the general scope of your project.
What do you want to accomplish? Frame the core idea.

For example: 'I want to find a mentor.' 'I want to redo my kitchen.' 'I want to make more money.' 'I want to get in better shape.' 'I want to establish the habit of daily meditation.' 'I want to learn to speak Italian.' 'I want to have a wonderful wedding.'

3. Identify the purpose of your project.
Why are you doing this? Be honest with yourself. Understand what's really motivating you. How compelling is it? 'I've got a book inside me and it feels like I'm going to burst until it's down

on paper' is different than 'I wanna be rich and famous' or 'Well, Phil wrote a book and if he can do it, I can do it.'

If you think about your true motivations, you may conclude that a different project is more appropriate at this time. When you find a project that truly moves you deep down—that connects with your core being—its purpose will feel important and meaningful. That kind of purpose will energize you. It will spark you into action and fuel you throughout the project.

Should you find your motivation flagging, you can remind yourself why you're doing this particular project. A fulfilling purpose will propel you back on course.

4. Refine the scope of your project.

Be as specific as possible. What *exactly* do you want to do? By when?

For example: 'I want to increase profits by 25% by the end of the year.' 'When I visit Rome next summer, I want to be able to converse with locals and find my way around.' 'I want to self-publish a 150-page tofu cookbook within ten months.' 'By my next birthday, I want to be doing fifty push-ups a day.'

5. Consider what has worked for you in the past.

Review your 'What Works for Me' list (Chapter 2). Remind yourself: When you tackled important projects in the past, how did you organize yourself?

Maybe you are more productive when you do your most important tasks first thing in the morning. Perhaps setting up weekly homework quotas got you through college. Or is it that you can do anything...if only you've got an accountability buddy?

Capitalize on what you already know about yourself and what works best for you to *get it done.*

6. Sketch out a general game plan for your project.

What needs to happen, in what order, by when? Include what you already know and identify what you don't. Consider the first steps and any other known action or foreseeable time constraint. If you are working toward a target deadline, start there and work backward to today.

Break it down into reasonable chunks. Identify some key milestones and deadlines along the way.

If your plans feel scary or overwhelming, break them down further into smaller and smaller pieces until you have a clear, calm picture of the simple action items required.

For example: 'Re-do my Kitchen' would break down into chunks such as 'budget', 'design', 'choose materials', and 'find a good contractor'.

If any chunk seems overwhelming, use the baby steps technique to break it into smaller pieces. 'Choose materials' might include steps such as 'Go to the library and look at books and magazines to get ideas of what I want'. 'Research appliances online'; 'Ask friends for recommendations'; 'Go to stores to see materials in person'; 'Pick cabinets'; 'Select flooring'; 'Choose a sink and faucet'; 'Pick paint'; 'Select knobs and other hardware'; 'Choose appliances'; 'For each item, find the best price'; and so on.

7. Review your initial game plan.

Is it reasonable? Practical? Doable? Motivating? Too challenging or too lax? Will life allow this plan?

Adjust your plan accordingly. You are trying to set yourself up for success—not stress yourself out. You've got enough stressors in your life already. Let your plan be 'reasonable' and 'achievable' instead of 'crazy-making'. Remember Key #1: Do less to get more done.

The ideal pace is to make steady progress such that you enjoy the process, are compelled to move forward, and delight in your victories along the way.

8. Enhance your plan.

Establish accountability. What will you do? What will others do? Identify what support you have available and what support you'll need to find.

What do you need to accomplish your plan? What's already in place? What's missing? How can you fill those gaps? Take a moment to consider each of the following:

- Information
- People
- Financial
- Technical
- Supplies and materials
- Communications
- Organization (e.g., how you will keep track of your project notes, ideas, materials, and progress)

REMEMBER: you don't have to know all the answers—you just need to ask the questions.

If you get stuck or stumped, consult others. Research answers online. Post a question via social media. Ask your colleagues, friends, and family for their ideas and suggestions. Ideally, brainstorm with a group of trusted, relevant others to get ideas popping.

Building on step one, set up a way to record all aspects of your project—your ideas, goals, plans, activities, costs, communications, and everything else—in one handy, easily accessible location. Ideally, you're seeking a handy, easy way to capture all thoughts and ideas about the project; to make notes about what you need to ask or discuss with whom; to keep track of what you've pitched to whom, when; and so forth. This might be via computer files or apps or just plain paper.

Personally, I like using hard cover journals for each project. It may seem old school but it's served me well for decades. I can write, sketch, colour code, glue in clippings and pictures, draw graphs and timelines, log communications and meetings—all without relying on electricity or risking electronic failures. (Having lost electronic files, had hard drives crashed, and lost all the data in an electronic organizer, I'm comfortable using Luddite methods to keep tabs on my most important projects.) These journals are easy to carry around, easy to shelve, and always at the ready. Tucked inside the front of each is a single piece of paper to represent the overview of the entire project—usually festooned with sticky notes (e.g., 'To-do Today', 'To-Do This Week', 'Questions', 'Needed Communications'.)

9. Identify potential obstacles and challenges you may face. Enhance the likelihood of your success by identifying and pre-preparing for obstacles and challenges you are likely to encounter.

I like to think of this step as an 'inoculation' because it's analogous to taking precautions to protect yourself from anticipated dangers before you go on a trip. Just as it's prudent to get a cholera shot before traipsing through sub-Saharan Africa, it's smart to pause and think about likely hazards that might impede your progress before you actually begin.

When you inoculate yourself, you are less likely to succumb to nefarious elements. Those who include this step in their planning are far, far more likely to succeed than those who don't.

What resistance can you expect? Brainstorm potential answers to each obstacle and challenge. For example, if you anticipate financial hurdles, you could give some forethought to how you could economize and raise revenue to attain your goal. If you foresee others' disapproval or jealousy diminishing your enthusiasm, you would do well to keep your project under wraps as long as possible. If you tend to have difficulty starting something new, you could apply whatever techniques work well for you to overcome it. (You could also turn to Chapter 6 for eight ways to get started.)

Based on my coaching work, I can tell you that the biggest obstacle you are likely to face is yourself. How do you get in your own way? How do you tend to sabotage yourself?

What do you need to watch out for as you embark on this project? What will you do when your inner saboteur arises?

ACTIVITY

INOCULATE YOURSELF FROM LIKELY OBSTACLES

Write out answers to the following questions:

- As you contemplate your project, what obstacles are likely to arise?
- In the past, what obstacles have arisen when you've tried to accomplish something?
- How do you tend to sabotage yourself? How do you get in your own way?

For each item in the preceding lists, brainstorm possible solutions. *If you get stuck, try researching options online or asking other people for their ideas.*

Keep this list handy, going forward.

10. Establish a process for regularly monitoring your progress. What are reasonable metrics to keep? What's the easiest way you can record your progress? It doesn't have to be onerous or a project unto itself.

For example, you could keep a project journal or jot tick marks on a calendar or keep track on a whiteboard, journal, or index cards. There are all manner of apps, websites, and software available to keep track of projects, if that appeals.

What will work for you to monitor your progress on this particular project? What's worked well for you in the past? Is there something new you'd like to try?

Also, identify rewards you can give yourself for your progress.

11. Conduct regular Progress Reviews.

A weekly or monthly five-minute check-in seems to work well for most people. During these brief sessions, ask:

- What have I accomplished?
- What worked well?
- What didn't?
- What adjustments need to be made?

As well, schedule longer, deeper Project Reviews several times throughout the year.

12. Schedule your first key actions and milestones as well as your first Progress Review.

Pull out your calendar or planner and assign particular tasks for specific times. Be sure to schedule your first steps and your first Progress Review, plus any known milestones, targets, or deadlines.

ACTIVITY

PLAN YOUR PROJECT

Set aside one hour of uninterrupted time to focus your attention on your top priority project.

Begin working your way through the planning steps in this chapter.

◆

How to Implement Your Plan for Your Project

Once you've selected your top priority and planned your project, the next step is to do it. Here's how:

1. Start.

With any new project, there's a natural excitement to get cracking, so there's usually a high motivation to begin. So go ahead. Start!

ACTIVITY

Right now, go do something to advance your project. (If in doubt, review your lists of First Steps and do whatever is easiest.)

If you did the activity, congratulations! You're on your way to *Get it Done*. Carry on to the next point.

If, however, you didn't, ask 'Why?' If you know, go ahead and address whatever it was that prevented you from starting. Then re-try the preceding activity again.

If you don't know—or if you tried again and still didn't start—turn to Chapter 6 for eight ways to get started.

2. Monitor and reward your progress.

From the get-go, make a practice to monitor and record your progress. On p. 69, you identified ways to keep track of what you're doing. Once you start, it's a matter of tracking your progress. Give yourself credit for every task, and every bit of time you spend on your progress.

Many people find the mere act of tracking their progress to be highly gratifying. It's pleasing to see we're actually doing what we set out to do. It motivates us to continue.

To supercharge your motivation, make a point of enjoying whatever rewards you identified as part of your planning.

This is where many people cheat. They don't reward themselves. They delay or deny themselves whatever simple pleasures they could be enjoying. Don't let this happen to you! You've done what you set out to do. You've earned a treat. Reward yourself.

If you consistently reward yourself for your progress, you are far more likely to continue with your project and you are far more likely to complete it. If you want to *Get it Done*, reward yourself for your progress.

3. Establish momentum.

It really doesn't matter *how much* you're doing, just as long as you are doing *something* consistently.

This is where the Magic Hour Method and the Baby Steps approach can be helpful. The best way to establish momentum is to focus on reasonable, doable small steps…and to keep doing them. The fact is, a journey of a thousand miles *will be* completed in only two hundred days, a little over six months, if you walk only five miles a day.

> ACTIVITY
>
> What schedule is reasonable and doable for you? How can you foster regular progress on your project? How can you make a firm commitment to the schedule you've chosen?

As soon as you get rolling, you'll experience the benefits of this slow-but-steady approach. Every session becomes an accomplishment. Your project becomes self-motivating and self-rewarding. Your enthusiasm and energy will flow even when you're not working on your project. Ideas will pop up all the time. Getting started during a given session will be easier and more fun than if you've abandoned your project for a time and have to start cold, asking, 'Okay, um, where was I?'

4. Keep going.

Once you establish momentum, focus on enjoying the experience. Cultivate a 'yay!' attitude towards the time you spend on your project—'I get to' or 'I want to'—rather than 'I have to' or 'I should'.

If at any point you feel like your project is an obligation or a millstone, something needs adjusting. No one is forcing you to do this, so why aren't you enjoying it? Turn to Chapter 8 to figure out what's going on and to make whatever adjustments are necessary.

As you move forward, pay attention to your progress and reward yourself accordingly.

Avoid the temptation to delay your rewards until you are 'done'.

Avoid focusing on the end product—or the distance between where you are and where you want to go. Doing so can be frustrating, de-motivating, and downright crazy-making.

To the extent you can shift focus to your progress, rather than any eventual product, the experience will be more positive and easier to keep going.

5. Make adjustments as needed.

The reason for having regular Progress Reviews is to identify what adjustments are needed so that you can correct your course sooner, rather than later.

No project hums along tickety-boo, with no surprises, from start to finish. Every enterprise encounters glitches and bumps along the way. It's important to be flexible in making necessary adjustments in response to whatever unfolds.

It may be that an obstacle arises that you anticipated as part of your plan. Address it with the solutions you prepared.

If something unexpected has arisen, do what makes sense. Once you've identified an issue, find a solution.

If you get stuck, research options or ask for ideas from others. Also refer to Chapter 8 for ways to overcome common obstacles.

6. Know when to say 'when'.

Sometimes you'll need to solve problems, sometimes you'll need to change course…and sometimes you'll need to pack it in. The trick is to recognize if it's time to move on…or if you're quitting prematurely for the wrong reasons.

If you're not sure if you should quit a particular project, turn to Chapter 9.

7. Finish.

Complete what you set out to do.

If this isn't your strong suit—if you need help pushing through that last five or ten percent—turn to Chapter 9.

And be sure to acknowledge what you finish. You've put all this effort into your project. Bask in your accomplishment. Savor it. Reward yourself. Avoid racing off to the next thing without first giving yourself your due.

◆

WHAT TO READ NEXT

I encourage you to pause reading now and go do your project. You are reading this book to get something done. You've chosen a project, and planned it. So go *get it done*.

Think of the remainder of this book as a troubleshooting guide. Fold down the top corner of this page so you can find it if issues arise as you embark on your project. Turn to the relevant chapter for solutions.

If you have trouble getting started—or if you find yourself procrastinating, turn to Chapter 6.

If you have difficulty staying on track, turn to Chapter 7.

If you have trouble overcoming obstacles that arise, turn to Chapter 8.

Turn to Chapter 9 if:

- You're grappling with whether or not to quit a project.
- Your project ends prematurely for reasons out of your control, or
- You are having difficulty actually finishing something you'd like to complete.

CHAPTER 6

Eight Ways to Get Started

Starting a new project can be thrilling—and scary. Exciting—and confusing. Overwhelming, too. It's not surprising that 'getting started' can be a challenge. Or that our clever unconscious minds often mask what's really going on.

Sheila recognizes her procrastination when she finds herself inexplicably snacking when she's not actually hungry. When Bart notices tell-tale signs such as his home is spotless and his files, books, and CDs are all alphabetized—then he knows he's avoiding doing something he needs to do. Terry knows she's putting off starting when she detects nervous 'butterflies' and has difficulty sitting still. Jack catches himself over-researching, spending excessive hours online instead of actually getting on with the task at hand.

What about you?

ACTIVITY

How do you know when you are procrastinating? What are the typical tell-tale signs that you are not getting started on something? Be candid.

As soon as you realize that you've been avoiding or resisting getting started, you can take action to begin. Here's how:

1. Review your original plan.

Pull out your projecting planning notes and ideas. Remind yourself why you wanted to do this project in the first place.

- What is your purpose in doing this project?
- What benefits do you foresee?
- What would it mean to you to complete this project?

2. Assess your current state.

Procrastination feels awful and takes a hefty toll. It's unpleasant and stress-inducing. It can make you feel bad about yourself. Left unchecked, it can harm your health and well-being.

- How does it feel when you procrastinate?
- How does procrastinating affect you (e.g., physically, psychologically, emotionally, or behaviourally)?
- What are the consequences of your procrastination?
- How does your procrastination affect people around you?
- What would it mean for you, personally, to start? How would it feel if you could start?
- How would you prefer to be operating? What is the spirit you'd like to bring to your project?

3. Identify baby steps forward.

Make it easy for you to start.

- What's the simplest, easiest thing you could do to move forward?
- How can you make this more pleasant for yourself?
- What has helped you get started in the past?

4. Schedule a reward for starting.

Identify a fitting treat for getting started—a walk, a special meal, fifteen minutes of cyberScrabble—whatever would be pleasant for you.

- What would be a pleasant, fitting reward for starting?

Note: You must actually treat yourself for starting.

5. Schedule a punishment for not starting.

It seems harsh to me but some people swear by this technique: They publicly promise to donate money to a cause they *don't* like, should they not fulfil their commitment to do something.

For example, you could make a public statement that if you don't start today, you will donate $500 to an organization you abhor.

- What would be an unpleasant punishment you could set up if you fail to start?

6. Make a public declaration to start.

Sometimes we need other people to help us start by holding us accountable. Phone, text, or email someone to say you're going to start. Post it on social media.

- Who could you contact who will hold you accountable?
- How might you use social media to hold you accountable? (And once you do start, report back as a way of rewarding your accomplishment.) If this works well for you, consider finding an accountability partner or group to help keep you on track, going forward. (More on this in Chapter 7.)

7. Use a timer.

Set a timer for ten minutes. Commit to doing as much as possible during those ten minutes. Whatever you get done is enough.

Bonus #1: You will also avoid distractions. Somehow, when the timer is ticking, it helps foster focus.

Bonus #2: You will be surprised how much you can accomplish when you give yourself a ten-minute time limit. There's something about the time pressure that motivates you to you get things done.

Bonus #3: When the timer goes off, it is likely that you won't want to stop. A body in motion stays in motion—sometimes we just need a little nudge to get the ball rolling.

8. Dig deeper.

If none of the preceding seven techniques get you started, dig deeper. What's really going on here? If you can't figure it out yourself, get help. Find a coach, a mentor, or a spiritual counsellor. Check out programs designed to overcome procrastination.

Once you get started, you need to stay on track. The next chapter provides six tools to do just that.

CHAPTER 7

Six Essential Tools to Stay on Track

Once you get started on your project, the next objective is to keep going. This is a challenge for many of us because of everything we have going on. It's very easy to be pulled in multiple directions, pretty much every day.

Sure, you intend to make those cold calls/take that Italian class/get to the gym...but then the car battery dies and your top client has an urgent deadline and your sister gets sick and your buddy needs a favour and suddenly it's Friday and you haven't spent five minutes on your most important project.

Embedded into earlier chapters of this book are six tools to keep you on track. We'll review and expand on them here.

Tool #1: Each morning, begin your day by choosing your top priorities.

Start each day by selecting a few key tasks that you *know* you can complete. Be swift and deliberate. Avoid taking more than two minutes to choose your day's priorities and to write them down.

There are many ways to do this. How you evaluate your options depends on your current situation. On the following page are examples of questions to choose your top priorities. It's up to you to decide which make the most sense for you on a given day.

- Which two or three tasks would be the most important for you today?
- Which two or three tasks would be the most gratifying or fulfilling for you today?

- Which two or three tasks would be the easiest for you to do today?
- Which two or three tasks would be the most fun for you today?
- Which two or three tasks would be the most exciting for you today?
- Which two or three tasks will allow you to learn and grow?
- Identify two or three areas of life you want to make progress in today (e.g., work, domestic, and health). Ask, 'What's one thing I could today to make progress in each area?'

Tool #2: Monitor your progress daily.

There is no short-cut. There is no getting around it. To keep on track, you must record and acknowledge whatever you get done on your project, every day. Yes, every day.

Make note when you complete your chosen priorities for the day. Also give yourself credit for everything else you do. If you have your project broken down in tasks, you could give yourself a check mark or star on any steps you took during the day. For example, if you're trying to get fitter, you could give yourself credit for things like:

- *Actually getting to the gym*
- *Every fifteen minutes spent in some physical activity*
- *Every glass of water you drink*
- *How many steps you take a day (measured with a pedometer or FitBit)*

Use the easiest way to track your progress. There are lots of apps available that you can download on your phone, tablet, or computer to set specific goals and track your progress daily. To find them, google 'goal tracking apps'.

Another option is to have an Accountability Buddy to whom you can report your progress—by phone, text, Zoom, or email.

Pick someone who makes your heart sing—someone you trust and find inspiring. The idea is to set regular goals and to keep yourself accountable.

This works particularly well when you partner with someone who shares similar goals. You can support each other and commiserate while keeping each other on track.

Or you can use your favorite social media outlet to tell the world what you've done. A fellow coach made tremendous progress in his fitness goals by doing precisely this. By posting his weight and daily fitness activities, he stayed committed—and publicly reporting his progress was intrinsically rewarding. 'As of this morning, I'm down 23 lbs from my starting weight!' It kept him on track...and frankly, it was nice for his followers. It's nice when you see someone succeeding ('I'm tickled for Brian—he looks great!') and it's also a helpful nudge ('Hmm, what attention am I giving my own body these days.')

If there's a way to chart your progress on a graph (e.g., amount of time/pages/product per session), do so. It's a visual, at-a-glance image of your progress. It might go up and down a bit but you can see the general trend, which can be motivating indeed.

If you haven't yet tried creating a nightly 'Ta Dah' List to chronicle your accomplishments, please do. It takes five minutes and feels fabulous. I highly recommend it.

Tool # 3: Set up weekly reminders.

In addition to chronicling your daily progress, it's helpful to set up external weekly reminders about your projects.

If you're keeping track of your daily progress, why bother with weekly reminders, too? Because it is so very easy for urgent items and random aspects of life to overtake your time and energy. By regularly reminding yourself about your projects, it's more likely you will keep them from being shoved aside by whatever life throws at you. Sure, you'll still need to attend to your car's sudden transmission woes/sick pet/needy friend...but you're more apt to attend to these things without abandoning your projects completely.

So how best to do this? Here are four easy, effective options to set up weekly reminders to keep you on track. Try any or all of them and see how they help you maintain momentum on your project.

Option A: Set up a Weekly Review.

Schedule five minutes at the end of each week. Use this appointment to remind yourself of your major projects and goals. Review the past week. Take a moment to note your accomplishments. Did you reward yourself for what you got done? If not, why not?

Next, ask yourself the following: What's working well? What's not? What adjustments can you make going forward? Give some thought to what's most important for you in the upcoming week.

Keep things simple and attainable. The idea is to motivate yourself—not to stress you out.

Option B: Find a relevant Mastermind group, support group, or weekly meeting.

If you find it hard to keep yourself accountable when left to your own devices, find help.

Is there an existing group you can join? This might be a Mastermind group, a trade or networking event (e.g., a writers' group), or a relevant program (e.g., if you want to trim down, you might join a fitness class or attend Overeater's Anonymous meetings).

If there isn't an existing group, can you find one or more Accountability Buddies? Can you gather together one or more people to help hold each other accountable? This might be in person or it might be via social media, Facetime, Zoom, email, or phone.

Whether you are connecting with one person or ten, the idea is for each person to state their intentions for the next week. Then, seven days later, 'fess up. How did you fare? What got done and what didn't? What adjustments do you need to make? What do you intend to do during the following week?

Option C: Sign up for relevant e-mail prompts.

The simplest, easiest way to receive weekly reminders is to subscribe to relevant, free weekly email prompts.

Prompts are automatic, free, and effective. They can be inspiring and helpful. Even if you don't open them, seeing them in your inbox will at least remind you of your priorities. If you do open them and take a few moments to process their contents, all the better.

As one of my subscribers told me, 'I do treasure these prompts. Sometimes they make me grumpy because I don't want to do anything but cope with what I have in the moment...which is usually precisely when I need to refocus and see the larger picture.' Another says, 'I find the advice focused, practical, quick to employ and ultimately effective. I appreciate any support that moves my work forward.'

Option D: Sign up for a class or two.

Whether you're teaching or taking them, classes provide you with a regularly scheduled date with your top priority as well as an opportunity to learn, grow, and hone your skills. Classes allow you to be exposed to new perspectives and to interact with like-minded people drawn to topics in which you're interested.

If you'd rather do it alone, then schedule regular time to focus on your projects—as if it was a private class. A block of time once or more a week can work wonders.

Tool # 4. Conduct regular Progress Reviews.

First, be sure to conduct your five-minute weekly check-ins.

As well, I encourage you to schedule longer, deeper Project Reviews several times throughout the year. The idea here is to pause and consider the Big Picture from time to time.

If you don't, life has a way of interfering with your progress. You can lose perspective and motivation. You can get stuck. Sometimes it's been so long since we worked on something, it takes a great deal of momentum to bring ourselves back up to speed, let alone proceed.

Sometimes entire projects become forgotten. Have you ever discovered a partially completed project...and you can't recall starting it, nor can you fathom why or when you stopped working on it? You are not alone.

To the extent that you can keep good track of your projects, you can avoid all these costs. Effective Project Reviews keep track of the Big Three—the time frame, scope, and resources—of our activities.

When you do so, you can get more done, more efficiently with less stress and less waste. You can put your time, efforts, and creativity to good use, rather than squander it. Regular Progress Reviews allow you to:

- Be aware of how far you've come over time
- Have a deeper understanding of your project
- Avoid missing deadlines or having things fall through the cracks

- Make better use of your time and resources
- Assess and manage risks as they arise
- Identify challenges and solve problems proactively
- Be able to communicate effectively about your project
- Avoid disorganization and inefficiency (e.g., can't find work you've already done…so you are forced to do it again, costing more time, effort, and resources)
- Maintain momentum and progress

The key is to schedule your Project Reviews well in advance. When each Project Review appointment rolls around, it's an opportunity to keep you on track.

Use the time frame that makes sense for you—be it monthly, quarterly, every six months, or annually. Block out thirty or sixty minutes of uninterrupted time for your Project Review.

Note that this might be a solo endeavour or it may be a team activity, depending on who are the relevant people in your project (e.g., team members, customers, colleagues, service providers, and key stakeholders.)

When it's time for your Project Review, begin with the Big Picture:

- What is the project's scope and purpose? Why do it?
- Where are you in the process? What's behind you and what's ahead?

Then focus on what's happened since your last Project Review:

- What's been accomplished?
- What's working well?
- What's not?
- What adjustments need to be made, going forward?
- What information is needed?

- What resources are needed (e.g., personnel, financial, technical, practical)?
- What goals or priorities make sense to target for the next Project Review?

Tool #5: Reward yourself for progress.

I talk about rewards a lot in this book because they work. When you actually give yourself treats for doing what you set out to do, you are more likely to keep yourself on track.

You might feel odd rewarding yourself for X when you've still got Y, Z, A, B, C, and D to do, but if you don't reward yourself now, you'll slow your progress. If you do reward yourself along the way, your project will unfold faster and more pleasantly.

Some of my coaching clients find it works well to give themselves points for certain things...then cashing in their points for fabulous prizes of their own devising (e.g., dinner out, a massage, concert tickets, a vacation).

For example, Sheila gave herself points for doing what she knew would help become a healthier version of herself so she could 'earn' new clothes.

5 points: re-reading my list of reasons/motivations to manage my weight
5 points: measuring ingredients for a meal so I know exactly what I'm consuming
10 points: eating a meal slowly and mindfully—away from the TV, computer, or other distractions
5 points: putting my fork down between bites
5 points: entering what I ate for my meal into my food journal

In Chapter 5 you were encouraged to identify particular milestones in your project and to select appropriate rewards for each. If you haven't already done so, take a moment to consider what treats you'd like to give yourself for which activities or milestones.

If you tend to short-change yourself in this area—if you tend to rush off to the next thing before acknowledging your achievements—here's an opportunity to change. Try treating yourself. See what effect it has on you, your project, your progress, and your motivation.

Tool # 6: Persistence.

Keep going. Keep taking steps forward.

There is no substitute or shortcut for persistence.

When you experience setbacks, learn what you can, regroup, and restart. (If you get stuck, turn to Chapter 8.)

Remind yourself what's worked well for you in the past. What helps you persist?

People who get things done persist. They keep starting and restarting and starting again. Consider these examples:

Colonel Harland Sanders' infamous chicken recipe was rejected 1,009 times before he found a restaurant to accept it.

Although Emily Dickinson only had a handful of poems published during her lifetime, she kept writing…leaving almost 1,800 completed works.

It took Thomas Edison over 1,000 tries to perfect the light bulb. He has been quoted as saying 'If I find 10,000 ways something won't work, I haven't failed. I'm not discouraged, because every wrong attempt discarded is often a step forward.'

Winston Churchill lost every election for public office in which he ran…until age sixty-two when he became prime minister of England.

For the early part of her career, Lucille Ball was denigrated as a 'B' movie star and a lousy actress. She persisted and eventually created an extremely successful television career.

When film critic Roger Ebert's cancer robbed him of the capacity to eat solid food, he went ahead and wrote the cookbook he'd always wanted to produce.

Jack London's first story was rejected six hundred times before the author of *Call of the Wild* and *White Fang* finally found a willing publisher.

R. H. Macy's first seven businesses failed before he created a successful enterprise in the form of Macy's department store.

When you encounter challenges, persist.

◆

To the extent you utilize the six tools in this chapter, you are more likely to stay on track. If you stay on track, you will *get it done.*

When you encounter obstacles, turn to Chapter 8 for ways to overcome them.

CHAPTER 8

Overcome Obstacles

As you take steps to *get it done*, it is likely that you will encounter obstacles along the way. Everyone experiences challenges. What differs is how different people deal with the obstacles they encounter. Some take it in stride and calmly move into 'problem solving' mode. (If that sounds like you, please skip ahead to the next chapter.) Other people panic or throw their hands in the air in despair or get thrown off track. If any of that sounds familiar, this chapter is for you.

Hopefully, you inoculated yourself against some potential obstacles as part of your planning process. If so, you have the opportunity to refer to the potential solutions you identified to overcome likely challenges, select an option, implement it, and carry on.

That sounds great in theory, but the truth is that when real obstacles arise, we tend to forget the obvious steps forward. I'm spelling them out here so you have them handy as a reminder to read when you are facing a challenge:

1. Expect the unexpected.

Going forward, know that unforeseen challenges and obstacles are likely to arise. When they do, acknowledge them, and move swiftly onto finding a way forward.

The sooner you can move from reaction *(Oh no! This terrible thing has happened! This is so unfair! The project is doomed!)* to action (*Okay, what can I do about it?*), the less likely you are to stall or get thrown off track.

2. Generate possible solutions.

When something goes awry, there's a natural tendency to pounce on the first solution you think of. That's good in that it moves you forward...but you may be missing out on a better way forward.

If possible, when you encounter an obstacle or challenge, pause to brainstorm ideas to overcome it. To the extent you consider different options, you are more likely to pick a better way forward.

The key here is to be brief. Set a time limit and generate as many ideas as you can. Be sure to generate some far-fetched options, for example:

- How would my grandparent solve this?
- How would a scientist solve this?
- What would a five-year-old do?
- How would my personal/professional hero respond?

Wanna supercharge your ideas? Ask trusted others to help you brainstorm possible solutions to your challenge. When two or more minds are devoted to solving the same problem, you will be capitalizing on the wisdom, perspectives, and experiences of others. Ideas can ping off each other into new and unforeseen solutions. You will devise a better way forward in a briefer period of time.

3. Evaluate your options.

Assess your possible solutions. If there isn't an obvious, single, best way forward, use a point system to rate the possible solutions you've generated. If something seems far-fetched, ask, 'Is there a kernel of an idea here that might work?' (*No, I can't advertise on the moon but what's a more practical, affordable location that a lot of people would see? Maybe I could advertise on social media.*)

4. Pick a solution.
Choose among the options. What makes the most sense for you, given your current circumstances?

5. Implement your solution.
Take action. The sooner the better. If in doubt, pick the easiest step you can take to implement your chosen solution.

6. Monitor your progress and adjust as needed.
From time to time, check in to assess how things are going. If your solution is working well, great. Carry on. Make note of any lessons learned. Reward yourself for finding an effective solution.

If you need to try something else, review your list of options and pick a different solution to implement.

◆

COMMON SETBACKS AND THEIR SOLUTIONS

No matter how well we plan and all the precautions we take to stay on track, sometimes our progress may become stalled or derailed. Here are four common ones:

Setback #1: Others Interfere
Sometimes people intend to support you…but may say or do things that obstruct your progress. And sometimes people interfere with your plans for random reasons.

If someone responds to your fitness efforts with something like, 'Why go to all that trouble? You don't really expect to get in shape at your age, do you?'—that's pretty overt, direct opposition to your plans. It's pretty easy to recognize and handle.

However, most interference is more subtle. Sometimes a lukewarm response to your plans is all that's needed to dampen your enthusiasm. Let's say you're all fired up about your new exercise program and when you tell someone about it, they say, 'Meh' and change the subject. That can quash your motivation and make you question the value of something that you've chosen as a priority.

Others' interference can be intentional or subconscious.

Let's say you're doing your darndest to shed some pounds and your partner keeps offering you ice cream or invites you out for a restaurant meal or comes home with armloads of your favourite junk food. Now your partner *may* be aware that these actions aren't helpful, but not necessarily. It could be that subconsciously, your partner doesn't want you to change because of a fear of losing you. Or maybe they don't want to feel pressured to go on a diet themselves. Perhaps, deep down, they are jealous of the progress you are making. Or maybe they just want you to be happy and you've been pretty cranky lately, given the food deprivation.

One thing to keep in mind is that the reactions of others may have little to do with you and much more to do with their own issues and challenges.

How to get back on track:

How you deal with interference by others will depend on the situation, the person, and your relationship to them. Use your good judgment.

If it's someone important to you, of course you'll talk about it. 'When you say or do [________], the impact on me is [_______]. I'd rather you say or do [______] because that would be more helpful.' *(When you buy junk food, it's frustrating for me. I'm trying to lose weight and having temptations in the house makes it more difficult. It'd help me if you would either avoid buying junk food or if you would keep it out of the house—like in your car or at your workplace.)*

If it's someone you don't trust, or someone who means little to you, you're probably better off saying nothing to them. Instead, remind yourself that they have no effect on you unless you let them

Regardless of who has interfered:

- **Remind yourself of your true motivation.**
- **Re-read your 'What Works Well for Me' lists.**
- **Be vigilant about monitoring your progress.**

ACTIVITY

Think of a time in which someone interfered with what you were trying to do, dampened your enthusiasm, or hampered your progress.

1. What did the person say or do?
2. How did you react?
3. What were the short-term and longer-term consequences?
4. How did you get back on track?
5. If you encounter a similar situation in the future, how would you like to handle it?

Setback #2: You Get Stuck, Stalled, or Derailed

Sometimes it can feel like you are spinning your wheels, getting too little done. It might be that you discover you're on the wrong path. Or you might find yourself blocked, paused, or at a dead stop.

Whenever you recognize you're being unproductive, pat yourself on the back. You noticed! Now you can do something about it.

How to get back on track:

- **Be kind to yourself.**

Avoid berating yourself for the situation. It doesn't help to be disappointed with yourself or to call yourself negative names. If you're reading this, you're a smart person with a lot going on. Give yourself some credit. Treat yourself as you would treat a friend in the same situation.

Know that we *all* have unproductive days sometimes. *Everyone* gets stuck or finds themselves off course at some point. It's human nature. *No one* is productive every hour of every day, every day of the week, every week of the year.

- **Assess the situation.**

Once you realize you're stalled, ask yourself, 'Why?'

Is it fear? Are you anxious about how things are unfolding? Are you concerned about something?

Is it fatigue? Do you need a mental or physical break?

Are you excessively stressed?

Is it that your project isn't going well and/or you've hit some vexing obstacle?

Is it that you are jumping around randomly between activities or projects without furthering any of them? Do you need to focus?

Has the well run dry? Are you lacking inspiration or motivation?

Is it that you are facing other challenges in life that are affecting your productivity? Is your life unbalanced?

Perhaps it's a combination of factors. What's your best guess about what's going on? If you're not sure, journal about it.

Putting pen to paper to describe the situation has a way of unlocking the truth.

- **Devise a course of action.**

Once you determine what's going on, you can do what makes sense: Face your fears, take a break, brainstorm solutions. What do you need to do to address whatever has caused you to become stuck, stalled, or derailed?

If in doubt, ask, 'What's the simplest, easiest thing I could do to move forward?'

Many of us tend to feel like 'it doesn't count' if we're not tackling complicated things. Doing anything less challenging can feel like 'cheating' or 'laziness'. This is a false belief that makes it difficult to get back on track because doing 'less' or doing something 'easy' feels wrong.

It's not wrong. In fact, it's completely necessary. If you're stuck, stalled, or derailed, allow yourself to do something easy for a change.

- **Remind yourself why you're doing this in the first place.**

What was your original motivation? Does that still apply? (If not, why are you beating yourself up, trying to do it?

Do something else.) If yes, what benefits are there to doing what you're doing? Literally write down as many reasons as you can.

Rekindle your original passion.

- **Choose to press the 'reset button'.**

Make a conscious decision to move forward. You can't do anything about the time you've squandered up to now. It's gone. But you *can* decide to change course going forward.

You have the right to a fresh start. Right now.

It doesn't matter what time of day it is. It doesn't matter what day of the week it is. It doesn't matter how long you've been unproductive. Right now, in this very moment, you can decide to change course.

You have power over this particular moment in time. You can choose to get unstuck, to get back on track, and to move forward.

As an added bonus, guess what? You can press the re-set

button more than once a day. (Some of us even have 'those' days during which we press the re-set button pretty much on the hour, every hour.)

- **Take action.**

Your initial goal should be simply to start. Something. Anything. Just start. Feel good about it. Avoid judging the size or significance of what you've done. Focus on any forward motion.

Don't believe me? Try this: Set a timer for ten minutes. Spend these ten minutes doing something—ANYTHING—to address whatever's been interfering. Focus on one thing. Do what you need to do: Make that scary phone call. Consult with a wise colleague. Take a baby step towards a solution. Take a nap. Organize your materials. Give yourself a change of scenery.

When the timer goes off, see how you feel. It's likely that even just ten minutes doing something will give you relief, motivation, and ideas to move forward.

- **Reward yourself.**

Once you start to move forward, be very, very proud of yourself. Any forward motion is to be appreciated and rewarded. Give yourself the treats you richly deserve.

- **Aim for gradual improvements.**

As you get going, continue to focus on forward progress. Build your momentum.

In all likelihood, once you get restarted, you'll accelerate your progress faster than you expect.

Setback #3: Life Intervenes

It is astonishing how often life intervenes when people embark on a particular course of action. Andrea pre-paid for a year at the gym and before she could go once, she fractured her fibula. John just started his diet and suddenly received three dinner party invitations. Kari began her Zen meditation practice and within weeks, her relatives descended on her, disrupting her newfound mindful calm.

Sometimes challenges arise in several areas of life in quick succession. For example, just after Karen started working on her MBA, she suddenly faced a tsunami of challenges. Her mother was diagnosed with cancer. Her husband asked for a divorce. Her daughter dropped out of college. She was forced to sell her house. She had to find a new job. That's a lot of challenges! It was a difficult period but Karen did get through it and was then able to resume her studies with a new wisdom and perspective she could apply to her studies.

How to get back on track:

- **Make good self-care your number one priority.**

Be kind and compassionate with yourself. If you don't take care of yourself first, you can't take care of anyone else who depends on you, nor can you deal with any of the things on your plate.

- **Accept what you can't change; change what you can.**

Understand that sometimes, unfortunately, bad things happen to good people. Bad things happen to everyone at some point, actually, so this is just part of life. You can't change the event but you can change your reaction to it.

- **Know that, whatever it is, you'll handle it.**

It may be unpleasant. It may be difficult. But you *will* get through this, just as you've gotten through everything else you've experienced thus far in life.

- **Adjust your timeline.**

It's okay to push back your plans. Return to them when possible. When it makes sense—when you believe that you're through the bulk of whatever you're dealing with—turn to Chapter 4 to reassess your priorities, then amend your plans accordingly.

Setback #4: Your Inner Enemy

In working with people over the past two decades, I've witnessed that the most challenging obstacles to getting things done come from within.

Do you have a little voice inside that is causing you damage? Do you have an inner saboteur that makes you doubt yourself, derail your progress, and/or otherwise create havoc in your life? If so, join the club.

Everyone—no matter how smart or successful—EVERYONE has one (or more) little tyrants inside of them that cause them to do things against their best interests.

Which of the following Inner Enemies interfere with your efforts to *get it done*?

THE FEAR MONGER

Anything new is scary to this Inner Enemy. Any change—even a good change—is regarded with anxiety and caution. On the plus side, The Fear Monger keeps us physically safe and prevents us from taking wild risks.

On the down side, The Fear Monger keeps us riddled with doubts and insecurities. It keeps us questioning our talents, rather than enjoying them. The Fear Monger sucks all the joy out of the task at hand. It keeps us paralyzed, fearing the future, rather than taking concrete actions today. The Fear Monger is particularly concerned about 'them' and what 'they' will say. (*What will the critics say? I can't write *that*! What will my mother say? What if my project bombs? I'll be a laughing stock. I'll never work again.*)

Also, The Fear Monger makes us demand constant reassurance from our friends, families, and colleagues. This can make us draining and unpleasant to be around.

THE DELAYER

Perhaps the cleverest inner saboteur, The Delayer can find untold impediments to block our progress. Symptoms may include a sudden urge to do chores. Or eat. Or nap. Or do more research. Or walk the dogs. Or surf the 'net. Or check Instagram.

The Delayer impedes our decision making. We find ourselves hesitating to commit to a particular choice or option, let alone take action along a particular path. The less we do, sadly, the more frustrated and unhappy we become. We berate ourselves. We feel weak and ineffective. We think poorly of ourselves. This is heartbreaking for people who care about us.

For others in our lives—especially coworkers—the delayer makes us undependable, difficult to work with, and often tardy.

THE JUDGE

The Judge is rarely satisfied. No matter what we do, our inner Judge knows we could have done it better. It's the voice in our heads intoning, 'This is not good enough.'

Ironically, we actually tend to do excellent work. Because The Judge is picky with sky-high standards, we tend to be conscientious, hard-working, and brilliant.

The downside is that we do so by putting tremendous stress

on ourselves and those around us. We assess every situation, every person, and every single thing we experience. We work frantically and joylessly, and seldom pause to acknowledge our accomplishments.

The people around us find it uncomfortable to share with us or work with us, knowing that we are apt to assess and critique them and their efforts.

THE DISTRACTOR

This inner saboteur is adept at finding cool new things to dangle in front of us. We just get going on a project when, suddenly, we are made aware of something new that hooks our interest. (We call this Bright Shiny Object Syndrome.) The Distractor is a master at scattering our efforts in random directions so we don't make sufficient progress in any one direction.

The Distractor keeps us very, very busy—our lives are interesting and full—yet we don't seem to be getting anything done, we don't feel particularly fulfilled, and we always seem to be running late.

Our friends, families, and colleagues get fatigued trying to stay abreast of whatever's captured our fancy today. They get irritated at our constantly shifting priorities (*Hang on. I thought we were doing X but now you want to do Y?*)

THE OVERCOMPLICATOR

This inner demon creates great drama out of simple situations. It can generate a thousand 'what if's' and complications for any scenario…none of which are very likely or relevant. It can devise convoluted rationalizations to talk you into—or out of—absolutely anything.

This whirlwind of our over-active, over-thinking minds can be bewildering, intimidating, or annoying to those around us. We can introduce new information or options at a time when it doesn't seem relevant to the task at hand. We can share too many ideas at once, making others confused or uncomfortable. We can inadvertently squash other people's input.

Without meaning to, The Overcomplicator can push people away. They may not want to disturb us or challenge us in the midst of a brainstorm. We can give off a negative vibe. Sometimes the wheels are turning happily in our brains and we're not aware of the position of our facial muscles. (This is especially true for smart women susceptible to 'Resting Bitch Face'. It's not fair but our society is such that if a woman's face looks tense or serious or the corners of their mouths aren't up, people tend to assume they are unhappy or negative or unpleasant and treat them accordingly.)

THE QUITTER

Have you had the experience of chipping away at something when you hit a roadblock? Then, before you can seek or implement solutions, The Quitter within wails in despair, 'We're doomed! We're done! We can't go on!'

We end up walking away from a perfectly viable project…or delaying its progress unduly. While The Quitter may make our lives easier in the short term, it dooms us to dissatisfaction and unhappiness in the long term.

The Quitter interferes with our efforts on things we actually yearn to do. When we don't do them, we feel guilty. We are plagued by regrets and disappointments and 'if only's'. We feel like failures. We can emit a 'loser' energy that is off-putting to others.

ACTIVITY

Re-read the descriptions of the Inner Enemies. For each, rate to what extent this is a problem for you. Use a scale of 1–10 in which '1' means 'not at all' and '10' means 'a lot'.

Highlight anything that seems particularly true for you. Add other examples from your own experience.

If one or more of these Inner Enemies is sabotaging your thoughts, work, or relationships, take heart. You are not alone. Everyone faces these inner demons at some point in life.

YOU, however, have the advantage of knowing what's going on. You can take action to combat these evil inner forces.

How to get back on track:

- **Understand your Inner Enemy.**

There's no need to be cross or frustrated with your Inner Enemy. Instead, be thankful. Your Inner Enemy is actually your brain trying to protect you from harm.

Understand that once you commit to do something, you've created a change in direction. Deep down, any change—even a positive change—is perceived at first to be threatening and dangerous by your subconscious mind. That's why your clever brain will seek ingenious ways to sabotage your progress.

Once you understand this, you can respond differently. For example, if you find yourself worrying about what 'they' might say, there is no need to berate yourself. Simply acknowledge what's going on. *(Oh, that's just The Fear Monger trying to prevent me from getting hurt.)*

Going forward, whenever you commit to a new path or project, prepare yourself. Keep on the lookout for signs of your

Inner Enemy—and understand that it's really trying to be your friend.

- **Detect your Inner Enemy.**

Given the sneaky nature of these inner saboteurs, the trick is to detect them. *(Hmm. Why haven't I picked up my banjo in a month? Good grief! The Delayer strikes again!)*

Going forward, be vigilant. Keep an eye out for your most persistent Inner Enemy.

Be attentive to what you are experiencing. If something feels unnecessarily fraught or stressful or complicated, pause and take stock. What are you thinking? What are you feeling? Ask yourself, 'Is this my Inner Enemy?'

Be very attentive to a little negative voice in your head. What is it saying? Does it sound like someone from your past?

Watch for cues from others. How are the people around you responding to your words and actions? Which Inner Enemy might be eliciting these reactions?

Each of us has our own preferred, well-practiced ways of resisting, cultivated from a lifetime of experiences. You know yourself best. How do you tend to sabotage yourself?

Left to his own devices, John is apt to quit prematurely. He's learned to watch out for this. If he finds himself unduly frustrated or self-critical or ready to throw in the towel, he reminds himself that it's just The Quitter within. He bargains with himself to keep going...just a while longer. Eventually, his inner resistance fades away.

Consider the following cues that may signal the presence of an Inner Enemy. Which are true for you?

- Laziness (*I just don't feel like doing this right now*)
- Confusion (*I just don't get this; This is too complicated*)

- Excessive thirst for information (*I can't start this until I do another month of research*)
- Fatigue (*I don't have the energy to tackle this; I need a nap*)
- Deferral (*I'll get around to this later/tomorrow/someday*)
- Excessive busy-ness (*I don't have time to do this; I've got too much going on*)
- Scattered efforts (*Gosh I better do X—no Y! No Z!*)
- Easily distracted (*Squirrel!*)
- Self-doubt (*I'm not good enough; I can't do this*)
- Dread or fear of the future (*What's going to happen?!*)
- Self-deprecation (*I don't deserve to succeed in this; I'm too young/old/stupid/serious/goofy/[fill in the blank] to do this*)
- Avoidance (*I'll just check my Facebook/email/phone messages; Hey look at this cat on YouTube; I really should clean the kitchen; Let me just see what's on TV*)
- Impatience (*Man, this is taking forever*)
- Despair (*What's the point? This is too difficult. I'll never make this better*)
- Self-medication (*Pass the tequila; Don't mind me as I shovel this bowl of popcorn down my gullet*)
- Quitting (*Ah, what's the point? I'll just pack it in*)

ACTIVITY

Re-read the preceding list. Highlight whatever is true for you.

- **Take stock.**

Once you are aware that an Inner Enemy is operating, dig deeper.

- What messages is the saboteur broadcasting in your brain?
- What actions are you taking because of it?
- What actions are you avoiding?

- What impact are you having on the people around you, personally and professionally?

The more specific you can be, the more opportunities you will have to combat your Inner Enemy.

ACTIVITY

1. Which Inner Enemy is causing you the most disruption right now? Name it.
2. Clear ten uninterrupted minutes to write out (or type out) answers to the following questions:
   - What are you feeling? *(E.g., fear, dismay, disappointment.)*
   - What is your Inner Enemy saying to you? What messages are you hearing?
   - What thoughts is it generating? *(If in doubt, scan your mind for any negative, painful statements about yourself or what you are doing.)*
   - What actions are you taking because of this Inner Enemy?
   - What actions are you avoiding because of it?
   - What impact is this Inner Enemy having on your personal relationships?
   - What impact is this Inner Enemy having on your professional relationships?

- **Take action.**

No matter which Inner Enemy is at work, ask, **'What is the simplest, easiest thing I could do to move forward on this?'** This deceptively simple question is designed to disrupt every Inner Enemy.

The Fear Monger dissipates with action. And action feels so much better than fear. Think of a time you were nervous to do something (speak in public, for example) but as soon as you began, your butterflies vanished. What a relief!

Similarly, The Delayer dissolves as soon as you start doing

something. (Anything!) If you have difficulty starting, turn to Chapter 6.

The Judge is pretty good about moving forward. **However,** you first need to suspend judgment about what you're doing. Understand that you can't accurately assess the quality of something while you're in the thick of it. Suspend judgment and keep going. If you hear negative inner messages (*This is crap!*), refute them (*I don't know that for sure. It might be fine. It might be great. I can't be sure at this point. I'll assess it later.*)

The Distractor is a reminder to channel your efforts in one specific direction. If you have difficulty deciding what to do, turn to Chapter 4.

The Overcomplicator is curtailed by the liberal use of the word 'easy'. Use this word as your magic wand. What's the *easiest* way to proceed? Do that. Then keep asking the question. What's the next easiest thing I can do? Go forward in the easiest way possible. If you are ever in doubt, pick what's easy.

If The Distractor or The Overcomplicator are at play, be sure to have a Park-it Pad handy to capture new ideas as they occur to you. There is no reason to drop what you're doing and race off in a random direction. Instead, just jot down the disrupting thought. It's safe and you can process it later. Now resume what you were doing.

If you're tempted by The Quitter, the action you can take is to ask, 'Is it really quitting time or is there something easy I could do?'

- **Look for effective countermeasures to curtail your Inner Enemy.**

The goal is to get into the swing of recognizing and countering your inner saboteurs as they arise. When you get adept at this, you may even laugh at them. *(Oh, there's ol' Distractor tempting me with another bright, shiny project. Nice try, D, but I'm going to finish the thing I'm working on first.)*

The best remedy for any of these Inner Enemies is purposeful, directed action.

If you are susceptible to a particular Inner Enemy, consider the following additional countermeasures.

To quell The Fear Monger:

- **What are you afraid of?**

When you detect that you are uncomfortable or afraid, it's helpful to identify the source(s) of your concern. Often this is a combination of factors. The best way I know to tease apart what's going on is through the activity below. The next time you detect the Fear Monger, try it.

ACTIVITY

1. Clear some uninterrupted time. As fast as you can, complete the following sentence fragments. Begin with the first one and complete it as many times as you can before moving onto the next.

   I'm nervous that…
   I worry about…
   I'm afraid that…
   I'm anxious about…
   I'm concerned that…
   I'm fearful that...
   I'm frightened that…
   I'm terrified of…

- **Address your fear.**

As soon as you begin to articulate your fears, congratulate yourself. You are among the few people who dare to do so.

Know that whatever discomfort arises, it is temporary. As soon as you identify a fear that is true for you, it's possible to address it. Here's how:

ACTIVITY

1. How does this fear affect your life? When does it arise? How does it affect you mentally, physically, socially, and otherwise?
2. How does this fear affect the people close to you?
3. What protection has this fear given you? How else has this fear served you well in your life? What benefits are you presently getting from this fear?
4. What is this fear costing you?
5. What would be the benefits of overcoming this fear?
6. Whose fear is this? Is this fear really yours, or is it the concern of someone else close to you—or of society as a whole?
7. Is this fear valid? Is it really true? What evidence is there to the contrary? What is the real truth here? What is the objective reality? Write out as many refutations as you can.
8. What would you rather believe? Be specific and detailed.

- **Is self-esteem an issue for you?**

If The Fear Monger is your constant companion, it may be affecting your self-esteem (i.e., how you see yourself) and/or your self-worth (i.e., how you value yourself). If so, know that there are proven ways to address these issues and to enhance your self-esteem.

Is a coach or counselor right for you? If you would prefer to work on this by yourself, there are many books available to help you build your self-worth and self-esteem.

To quell The Delayer:

- **Pick any way forward.**

If you find yourself in 'decision paralysis'—as if you can't move forward for fear of choosing the 'wrong' thing—review the prioritization techniques in Chapter 4.

It really doesn't matter what you choose. Pick something—anything—and take action. ANY action will feel better than being stuck.

If in doubt, pick the easiest way forward. Think of possible baby steps (pp. 19–20). What's the tiniest, laughably easiest action you could take?

- **Start.**

All you have to do is start. You don't have to finish. Just commit to beginning. If you need help, review Chapter 6.

To quell The Judge:

- **Suspend judgment.**

When you notice yourself evaluating or assessing someone or something, stop.

- **Consider that your judgment might not be correct.**

Your opinion is just your opinion. It may have little basis in reality.

This situation just 'is'. From your limited point of view, you have no accurate way of assessing if this situation is 'good' or 'bad' or 'scary' or anything else. What seems like a terrific opportunity at first blush might end up, in the long term, being the worst experience of your life. Something that appears to be a massive setback might in fact be a way for you to deepen relationships and devise a better solution that yields a far more successful project.

For example, let's say a gallery offers to exhibit your work. That seems 'good,' right? Now imagine that there's a fire in the gallery and a lot of your work is lost. Now your exhibition seems 'bad', right? But wait—because of the fire, let's say that you now get a lot of press and new commissions...well then, the original ill-fated exhibition seems 'good'. But what if you can't handle your newfound fame or you get swindled by unscrupulous financial managers or...you get the idea.

- **Generate alternatives.**

Whenever you notice yourself making a judgment, brainstorm a minimum of three other possible ways of reframing your original assessment. (Bonus points if you can make yourself laugh.)

For example, if your knee-jerk thought is something like, 'Wow, what an awful outfit Taylor is wearing,' consider some alternative interpretations:

(a) Taylor is dressing the best she can, given her pocketbook and taste.

(b) Taylor may be a fashion maven who is expressing herself in ways you're not appreciating.

(c) Taylor is so frazzled at work and home that she threw on whatever she had at hand and you're lucky she remembered to don her pants at all, and/or

(d) Taylor doesn't care a hoot about how her outfit looks so why should you?

- **Are you a Perfectionist?**

Is The Judge a chronic influencer in your life? Are you picky, with sky-high standards? Are you a bit of a control freak? You just might be a perfectionist. You may be putting yourself and those around you under undue stress.

Many perfectionists benefit from the help of 'neutral party'—a coach or counselor—to help them identify the toll of their perfectionism and to develop new ways of operating. If you would prefer to work on this by yourself, there are many books available to help you overcome perfectionism.

To quell The Distractor:

- **Identity and reduce distractions.**

Begin with the obvious. What's interfering with your focus? Remove it or reduce it.

- **Focus.**

Pick one thing and give it your full attention. When competing ideas arise, park them.

- **Train your Monkey Mind.**

You don't have to be held hostage by the ideas pinging around your brain. It's possible to learn to control and manage your thoughts through techniques such as meditation. It can be as quick and easy as pausing two or three times a day to use the following technique.

MINI-MEDITATION

Set a timer for three minutes. Close your eyes, focus on your breathing, and just be.

As your thoughts drift (and they will), simply nudge them aside and return your focus to your breathing.

If it helps, count. Or repeat a key word (such as peace or joy or 'om'). Or imagine the sounds of ocean waves in synch with your breathing.

- **Learn more about meditation.**

There are countless apps, books, and websites available to help you meditate. Not only will you be countering The Distractor, you will accrue many proven health and psychological benefits.

To quell The Overcomplicator:

- **Be aware of your triggers.**

What kinds of things do you experience when you over-think things? What triggers you to over-think things?

Think of a specific instance when you over-complicated a situation. What happened? How did you feel? What were the consequences?

Thinking back on it now, what might have been a simpler way forward?

- **Ask 'Am I over-thinking this?'**

Be attentive to what you are experiencing. If something feels unnecessarily fraught or difficult or complicated, pause and take stock. What is the truth here? What is the objective reality?

- **Watch for cues from others.**

What do you notice in the people around you when you over-think or over-complicate things?

Be attentive to the impact of your busy mind on people around you. They may well love your contributions...but there's probably a limit. Reel in the need to express every thought, idea, and option that crosses your cranium. Edit what you share and how you share it. Consider pausing five seconds before you speak.

- **When possible, simplify.**

Many roads lead to Rome. There are many, many ways to do anything. If something seems over-complicated—if you're mired in too many details and contingencies—ask, 'Is there a simpler or easier way forward?'

- **Establish a regular meditation practice.**

You would also benefit from training your Monkey Mind. To the extent you can establish a regular meditation practice, you can harness your analytical brain and direct it more effectively.

To quell The Quitter:

- **Remind yourself of your motivation.**

Why are you doing this in the first place?

- **Do something easy.**

If you can do something —anything—to move forward, do so. If you're at a genuine crossroads and need to decide whether or not to pack it in, turn to Chapter 9.

CHAPTER 9

Finishing

Starting is relatively simple. You just begin. Any step forward counts as 'starting'.

In contrast, finishing can be complicated. It can be riddled with emotions and confusion. Mid-way through something, it can be unclear if it makes sense to go on. When the end is nigh, it can be very tempting to run off to the next thing without actually completing what you intended...or without finishing well.

This chapter is for you if:

- You're trying to decide whether or not to quit a project.
- Your project ends prematurely for reasons out of your control.
- You decide to quit a project, mid-way through.
- You choose to finish but are having difficulty actually completing that last five or ten percent.
- You would like to finish your project well.

We'll address each of these in turn.

HOW TO KNOW WHEN TO QUIT

We've all been there—at a crossroads with our project, wondering whether or not to proceed.

When you are in that situation, the first thing is to discern if the issue is with you or with the project.

First, consider your own state. What's going on with you? What is your energy level? Are you fatigued? Consider your emotional state. Are you bored? Are you afraid? Are you depressed? Are you overwhelmed? Is an Inner Enemy at play?

It may be that you need a break. Or to get re-energized. Or to find some support. Or it could be that you've gotten what you needed to from this particular project and it's time to move on.

Next, consider the project itself. Remind yourself of why you started this in the first place. What were to be the benefits of this project? Are you getting out of it what you intended?

Does the project still interest you? Does the project still serve you? If not, why are you feeling differently about it? Have you suffered a setback in the project? Are you stuck? Do you know how to proceed?

What are the consequences of proceeding?

What are the consequences of packing in this project? If you don't finish it, will you regret it ten years from now? Will you regret it on your deathbed?

Is another project or activity competing? If so, which is more important or interesting to you at this point in time? If you need help deciding, prioritize.

As well, know that it's okay to choose to quit if that's what makes sense for you. There is no law compelling you to finish. No one has to finish *everything* they start. In fact, the physical reality is that it's absolutely impossible to do so.

So given all this, do what makes sense to you. **Choose to continue or choose to quit.** Be purposeful. If you decide to proceed, brainstorm solutions for whatever has interfered. If you opt to quit, do it well.

ACTIVITY

Consider a project that's been languishing for a while. Clear some uninterrupted time to answer the following questions:

- Is the issue with you or with the project?
- Is there something going on with you that is interfering with your progress on this project?
    - What is your energy level? Are you fatigued?
    - What is your emotional state?
    - Are you bored?
    - Are you afraid?
    - Are you depressed?
    - Are you overwhelmed?
    - Is an Inner Enemy at play?

Consider the project:

- Remind yourself why you started this in the first place. What were to be the benefits of this project?
- Are you getting what you intended out of the project?
- Does the project still interest you? Does the project still serve you? Why are you feeling differently about it?
- Have you suffered a setback in the project? Are you stuck? Do you know how to proceed?

- What are the consequences of proceeding?
- What are the consequences of packing it in? If you don't finish it, will you regret it ten years from now? Will you regret it on your deathbed?
- Is another project or activity competing? If so, which is more important or interesting?

Now, given all this, make a purposeful decision. Choose to continue or choose to quit.

WHAT TO DO WHEN YOUR PROJECT ENDS PREMATURELY

Sometimes we quit a project...and other times a project quits us. We might still be committed to it, but it gets taken away from us or it goes up in flames or comes to an end before we would like.

When this happens, it's natural to have an emotional response. You might be upset or disappointed or angry or frustrated or sad. Go ahead and grieve.

However, to the extent possible, avoid getting stuck in this negative state. Put a time limit on your reaction.

Then take steps to conclude your involvement with purpose. It might not have been your choice to end it, but you can still end it well.

Another important point: When a project ends prematurely, it is not a failure. Avoid treating it as such. Instead of griping about 'wasted time' or 'wasted energy' or 'what might have been,' value the experience of working on the project for the time you did. What good came out of it? What did you learn?

Believe me, I understand the temptation to despair. Here's my favorite example: I had spent a dozen hours making a complicated silver ring in a metalworking class. It was *almost* done…and when I was soldering it together, I accidentally melted the metal into an unsalvageable puddle. I burst into tears.

'Weeks wasted!' I wailed and proceeded to berate myself accordingly.

My sage teacher took me aside and pointed out, correctly, that:

(a) The point of taking the class was to acquire skills, experience and knowledge…not to produce particular products.

(b) The time and energy I had put into the ring was not, in fact, wasted. I had learned a lot during the process. (And I learned a heckuva lot more because of the psychological processing sparked by melting my ring—things I'm now passing onto you.)
(c) I've wasted much more time on much less important, less interesting activities in my life. The dozen hours spent on the ring that-wouldn't-be was a relatively short investment in a comparatively interesting activity.

This was a turning point for me. I hadn't realized how focused I'd been on the final product…and how dismissive of the experience—a process that I do truly enjoy.

As a result, I learned to cultivate a far healthier attitude to my metal projects. I shifted focus away from the target products and towards the experience of honing skills. I kept studying new techniques and came to expect apparent setbacks as an essential part of the learning process.

◆

HOW TO QUIT A PROJECT MID-WAY THROUGH

It doesn't matter why you are leaving a project unfinished—whether it has ended prematurely or if you've chosen to stop mid-way through—when it's time to quit a project, do so deliberately and respectfully.

1. Recognize that your involvement has concluded.
Make a clear and firm termination of your efforts.

2. Review your experience.
Consider what good has come out of it. What worked well? What

did you learn? What can you carry forward?

What didn't work well? What would you like to avoid repeating in the future?

3. Put away your project notes and materials.

Keep what you want. File notes that might be helpful in the future. Perhaps there's a memento you'd like to keep to commemorate this project—a photo or an object or something else? Put it aside as a positive memory of your experience.

Author Barbara Sher recommends packing up your half-done projects in small boxes or binders and adding them to a 'project shelf'—a shrine-like collection of former projects.

4. Jettison what you no longer need.

Do what makes sense with unwanted leftover materials. If you're not going to use something, sell it, donate it to someone who will get use out of it, or throw it away.

Above all else, get rid of any guilt or bad feelings about the project. It's done. It's over. Avoid dwelling negatively on it. Fixating on 'what if's' or 'if only's' doesn't help you. It just keeps you stuck in an unhappy, unfulfilled state.

Instead, take whatever good you can from the experience and move forward.

5. Let it go.

Make a positive, conscious choice to leave this project behind. The easiest way to do this is to start something new. Turn to Chapter 4 to select your next priority. Given your current situation, what would you like to do next? Put your thoughts and energy into moving forward.

◆

FINISHING—COMMON CHALLENGES AND THEIR SOLUTIONS

Often, simply choosing to finish something is enough to carry you through to completion.

However, sometimes we get snagged just before the end. Here are four common challenges people have in finishing...and what to do about each.

Challenge #1: Completing the Final 5%–10%

It doesn't matter how long or involved a project is, there can be a tendency to grind to a halt just short of completion. Sometimes it's mentally and physically difficult to keep going right to the end.

How can you keep yourself from stopping short?

Solutions:

- Remind yourself of your motivation for doing this project in the first place. What will it mean to you to finish?
- Look at The Big Picture. Remind yourself of your progress thus far. What have you already done? See how little is left to do, in comparison to what you've already accomplished?
- Bargain with yourself. For example, pick a minimum time to work on your project. Give yourself a reward for doing so.
- Review your 'What Works Well for Me' lists. What can you apply to your current circumstances?
- See if any Inner Enemy is at play. Are you Delaying or Overcomplicating things unnecessarily? Take steps to quell any Inner Enemy you detect.
- Ask others to hold you accountable.

- Make a public declaration that you will finish by a particular day. (Social media is great for this.)
- Pre-plan a big party for your target deadline. (It's embarrassing to have a wrap party if the film is still shooting.)
- Arrange a reward for yourself, providing you finish.
- Make a public declaration that if you *don't* finish by a particular day, you will donate a substantial amount to a cause you *don't* support.

Challenge #2: Fear of Loss, Premature Grieving

Sometimes, when we're heading to the home stretch on a project, we become filled with sadness…it's like the tears at the end of summer camp, knowing that you'll be missing the people and activities on which you've been focused.

Or you may feel concern about what will fill the void of this project, after it's done.

Solutions:

- Understand what's going on. It's natural and valid to mourn losses. Acknowledge the people, places, and activities you will miss at the conclusion of your project.
- To what extent can you carry forward some aspects of this project to your next endeavours? What easy, practical ways can you stay in touch with people with whom you don't wish to lose contact?
- Take some time to revisit Chapter 4. Pick what you'd like to do next so you know you'll have something interesting to turn to after you're done with your current project.
- If you are feeling anxious or fearful, take steps to quell your inner Fear Monger.

Challenge #3: Bright Shiny Object Syndrome

About the time you're almost done, you might get distracted by the Next Bright Shiny Idea to come along. It's new, it's exciting, and it sweeps your attention away from the more familiar project on which you've been working.

Solutions:

- Review how to quell the Distractor.
- When you notice yourself shifting focus to something new, pause. Use the Prioritization process to choose which project is truly more important to you at this time.
- If your current project is more important, remind yourself why. Rekindle your commitment. Push through the last five to ten percent. Park the Bright Shiny Idea somewhere safe and promise it to yourself as a treat when you've completed your current project.
- If the new project seems more important, verify this by working through the activity on page 119. If it's truly time to quit, do so purposefully (pp. 121–22) and move on.

Challenge #4: Perfectionism

If you find that last five percent takes as much time and effort as the whole rest of the project, you're probably tinkering a wee bit too much, striving for a 'perfect' product. Alas, there's no such thing.

As Pixar's Chief Creative Officer, John Lasseter, has said: 'Our films are never finished—they're just released.' If that approach works for the makers of *Toy Story, Wall-E, Up, Finding Nemo, The Incredibles* and other Oscar-worthy films, isn't it good enough for you?

Solutions:

- Keep in mind the 80:20 rule. Keep yourself accountable. Are you spending excessive time for minimal improvements?
- Realize that whatever you're working on will never be perfect. Allow it to be 'good enough'. Pick an end date and stick to it. Be like Pixar and 'release' your work, rather than finish it.
- Take steps to quell your inner Judge. Consider including a flaw on purpose—like the carpet weavers who intentionally include an imperfection in their masterpieces.

HOW TO FINISH WELL

How do you finish your projects? Do you celebrate and reward your accomplishments or do you race right into the next thing?

Often, we have so much going on that whatever we finish is overshadowed by our many as-of-yet-undone ideas and projects.

Looking at this tsunami of things on our To-do lists, it can be challenging to allow ourselves a victory lap. ('I can't stop for a party, now! I have too much more to do!')

Yes, it can be challenging—and it's important to finish well. When you acknowledge and celebrate what you finish:

- You give yourself the gift of experiencing fulfilment, accomplishment, and gratification.
- You have the opportunity to acknowledge and appreciate the efforts of everyone who has assisted you.
- You reinforce whatever actions or habits contributed to your success, which bolsters your future productivity.

- You boost your motivation for whatever you choose to do next.

In contrast, when you shortchange your accomplishments—or scrimp on celebrating them—you are basically devaluing what you do.

You're training yourself to toil without relief or reward—which is fatiguing and demotivating. You're running on the proverbial hamster wheel with no end in sight. There's only so long you can do this without it eroding your productivity.

You're also devaluing the efforts of whoever helped you. If you push onto the next thing without properly recognizing their contributions, how likely will they be to help you in future endeavours?

Luckily, it's simple and easy to avoid these costs. Whatever you finish, finish it well.

Here's how:

1. Reward your efforts with a private celebration.

Give yourself a treat to mark the conclusion of your efforts. Pat yourself on the back. Do what makes sense for you, given your personal preferences and circumstances. You might pour yourself a glass of champagne or buy yourself a fitting reward. You could take a soothing walk in nature or enjoy a fun daytrip. Maybe you choose to take a restful, pampering personal day—or go on a true vacation.

2. Take some time for private reflection.

Journal about your project. What thoughts and feelings do you have about it?

What does finishing this project mean to you? What went well? What didn't? What did you learn? What would you do differently, next time?

3. Plan a public celebration.

Find a way to acknowledge your efforts and accomplishments publicly.

If you feel so inclined, you could spread the good news via email or social media.

If possible, organize an event. This might be a party or a special meal with relevant others. What would be a fitting celebration?

4. Acknowledge the support you've received.

Whenever you finish something, you have an opportunity to recognize and thank friends, colleagues, and loved ones who supported your efforts. Give credit where credit is due.

Involve the people that helped you in the celebration. Allow them to share your success.

Are there any gifts or tokens of your appreciation you'd like to give?

MOVING FORWARD

Remember: you are a competent person who has accomplished many things in the past—and who has the opportunity to accomplish many things in the future. Hopefully, you've found the activities in this book helpful to get things done—and to do so easily, with less stress. The main emphasis has been on how to go forward in a way that capitalizes on your natural skills and preferences—to utilize what works for you and to avoid what does not—while quelling self-sabotage.

If something feels too stressful or fraught, pause and assess what is going on.

Are you straying from your 'What Works for Me' lists (Chapter 2)?

Are you trying to do too much? **Do less to get more done.**

Are you stuck? Ask yourself, **"What is the simplest, easiest thing I could do to move forward on this?"**

Are you multitasking? **Focus on one thing at a time** and you will make more progress on every activity.

Is your life feeling out of control? Utilize **time management strategies** that you know work for you (Chapter 3).

If you find yourself having difficulty priotizing or choosing what to do, turn to Chapter 4.

If you need a refresher in formulating practical plans, turn to Chapter 5.

If you are having difficulty getting started, turn to Chapter 6.

If you find it challenging to stay on track, turn to Chapter 7.

Should obstacles arise—especially one or more Inner Enemies—turn to Chapter 8.

If you are contemplating quitting a project, or nearing the end, turn to Chapter 9.

Wishing you all the best in all you do,
Liisa Kyle, PhD.

Acknowledgements

Heartfelt thanks to my coaching clients for their stories and contributions to the material in this book.

Grateful thanks to Janna Stewart and Paula Gill for reading earlier drafts of this book. Your detailed expert insights, feedback, and suggestions for improvement are much appreciated.

In gratitude for many blessings, a portion of the proceeds of this book is being donated to charity.